www.wadsworth.com

wadsworth.com is the World Wide Web site for Wadsworth and is your direct source to dozens of online resources.

At *wadsworth.com* you can find out about supplements, demonstration software, and student resources. You can also send email to many of our authors and preview new publications and exciting new technologies.

wadsworth.com
Changing the way the world learns®

ANDREW CARNEGIE
ROBBER BARON AS AMERICAN HERO

James T. Baker
Western Kentucky University

A collection of paradoxes, this man of American steel—he showed himself violent and peace loving, ruthless and loyal, greedy and generous, boastful and diffident, vain and doubting, brash and shy. Like his adopted country and so many of its citizens past and present, he exhibited a curious mixture of Jeffersonian rhetoric and Hamiltonian action. In his life we may easily see reflections of ourselves and our past.

HAROLD LIVESAY
Andrew Carnegie and the Rise of Big Business

WADSWORTH

THOMSON LEARNING ™   Australia • Canada • Mexico • Singapore • Spain • United Kingdom • United States

WADSWORTH

TM

THOMSON LEARNING

Publisher/Executive Editor, History: *Clark Baxter*
Development Editor: *Margaret McAndrew Beasley*
Assistant Editor: *Julie Iannacchino*
Editorial Assistant: *Jonathan Katz*
Technology Project Manager: *Jennifer Ellis*
Marketing Manager: *Caroline Croley*
Project Manager, Editorial Production: *Matt Ballantyne*
Print/Media Buyer: *Tandra Jorgensen*

Text Designer: *Adriane Bosworth*
Permissions Editor: *Joobee Lee*
Copy Editor: *Alan DeNiro*
Cover Designer: *Carole Lawson*
Compositor: *Buuji, Inc.*
Text and Cover Printer: *Transcontinental*
Cover Images: front cover portrait © *CORBIS;* art museum © *Richard Cummings/CORBIS;* steel factory courtesy *PhotoDisc;* back cover portrait © *Bettmann/CORBIS*

Printed in Canada
1 2 3 4 5 6 7 06 05 04 03 02

For more information about our products, contact us at:
Thomson Learning Academic Resource Center
1-800-423-0563

For permission to use material from this text, contact us by:
Phone: 1-800-730-2214   Fax: 1-800-730-2215
Web: http://www.thomsonrights.com

Wadsworth/Thomson Learning
10 Davis Drive
Belmont, CA 94002-3098
USA

Asia
Thomson Learning
60 Albert Street, #15-01
Albert Complex
Singapore 189969

Australia
Nelson Thomson Learning
102 Dodds Street
South Melbourne, Victoria 3205
Australia

Canada
Nelson Thomson Learning
1120 Birchmount Road
Toronto, Ontario M1K 5G4
Canada

Europe/Middle East/Africa
Thomson Learning
Berkshire House
168-173 High Holborn
London WC1V 7AA
United Kingdom

Latin America
Thomson Learning
Seneca, 53
Colonia Polanco
11560 Mexico D.F.
Mexico

Spain
Paraninfo Thomson Learning
Calle/Magallanes, 25
28015 Madrid, Spain

Library of Congress Cataloging-in-Publication Data
Baker, James Thomas.
 Andrew Carnegie: robber baron as American hero / James T. Baker.
  p. cm.—(Creators of the American mind; v. 4)
 Includes bibliographical references.
 ISBN 0-15-500011-X
 1. Carnegie, Andrew, 1835–1919.
2. Industrialists—United States—Biography.
3. Philanthropists—United States—Biography.
I. Title. II. Series.

CT275.C3 B35 2002
338.7'672'092—dc21
[B]   2001056817

For Christopher
———

CONTENTS

PREFACE

Scholars who spend their lives observing the phenomenon called the United States of America are intrigued by the question of whether there is an American mind. Some argue that the United States is too diverse, too complicated, too multicultural to have anything approaching a common way of thinking. Others, while not denying the great racial, regional, religious, ethnic, and cultural differences that divide Americans, still believe that there is a particularly American way of looking at the world, assessing issues, and acting on common principles, thus in fact demonstrating an American mind. These scholars emphasize the common history that Americans share, despite regional and local variations; the common dreams that Americans share, despite ethnic and cultural variations; and the common concerns Americans share, despite religious, social, and economic variations. Even when Americans quarrel, an elusive yet verifiable American mind provides them with common subjects to debate and common forms of ammunition for their arguments.

If there is indeed an American mind, it seems logical to suppose that along with historical events, certain individuals (political, religious, and intellectual leaders, male and female, of all ethnic, social, and economic groups) have through their thoughts, words, and deeds helped create it. Whether we admire, despise, or remain ignorant about what these persons said and did, their thoughts and actions have left an imprint on our history. This series, Creators of the American Mind, spotlights some of those important persons, listening where possible to their own words, comparing the sometimes conflicting opinions about them by their contemporaries and their biographers, and juxtaposing their supporters and critics and those influenced by them; all in an attempt to see how, why, and to what degree each one contributed to the development of the American mind.

The subject of this volume, Andrew Carnegie, an "adopted" American, is certainly a pivotal, central figure, a principle actor in the drama of American history. He might well serve as a test case for the theory of an American mind. If there *is* such a thing, Carnegie (and several other men of his generation and socioeconomic status) certainly helped create it. This book, I believe, offers a historically solid yet novel approach to Andrew Carnegie and his place in American history.

1.   It places Carnegie in historical perspective by following his rise from poverty in his native Scotland to his immigration to the United States, his success as an entrepreneur, his mastery of industry and finance to the point where he was for a time the richest man in the world, and finally his efforts as a philanthropist to give most of his fortune away. It demonstrates that he was in many ways much like his contemporary "robber barons" and yet with a philosophical, literary, and humanistic bent very uncharacteristic of most of them. It highlights Carnegie in order to demonstrate the strengths and weaknesses of the period Mark Twain named "The Gilded Age."

2.   It permits on Carnegie to speak for himself: to describe his rise from "rags to riches," which made him an American ideal; his reign as "the king of steel," which made him an American icon; the shameful episode of the Homestead strike, which exposed a side of Carnegie and his empire he tried always to conceal and deny, making him in some eyes an American disgrace; and his late career as a philanthropist, which made him seem to many people an American saint. Carnegie was certainly the most literate and articulate of the nineteenth-century men of wealth, and in the selections chosen for this volume he makes clear what he wanted the public to think of him—whether it was true or not.

3.   It demonstrates, through selections from his contemporaries, why and how Carnegie and the Carnegie image became such an integral part of the American way of thinking. It provides both factual and fictional commentaries that show how the images of the poor boy who made good, the powerful baron of business, the man of great wealth who tried to help humanity, permeated Carnegie's age—and our own as well. It also includes indictments of Carnegie, his policies, and his accomplishments by those who opposed him and his self-aggrandizement.

4.   It provides the sober, reflective analyses of several prominent scholars who have carefully taken stock of Carnegie and his achievements. These scholars, mostly historians, with whom students are here able to "rub shoulders," provide a valuable balance both to the worshipful hymns of praise from Carnegie's admirers and the blasts of contempt from his detractors. Their analyses should help students to see Carnegie the way historians see him and in the process learn historical methods and techniques.

5. It makes its historical material relevant and attractive to students by identifying contemporary figures, success stories, tycoons, strike breakers, and philanthropists—modern versions, in some form or another, of Andrew Carnegie. Whether students admire or despise these figures, they will be intrigued to read them in their own words as they share their tips for success, demonstrate how they keep the Carnegie tradition alive, and by those tips and comments add their bit to the creation of the American mind.

6. It offers, at appropriate intervals, analyses of the material being examined, summations of that material, and questions that teachers and students may use for critical, reflective essays or discussions of the major topics of the study.

7. It offers at the end a number of topics that may be used for extended papers on subjects central to the themes of the book. Under one cover there is enough information on these topics to write on Carnegie as a success story, as a captain of industry, as a "robber baron," as a philanthropist.

8. It provides an annotated bibliography on Carnegie and related subjects so that students may delve more deeply into areas of Carnegie's life and times that are covered only briefly or merely suggested in the book itself. Using the sources recommended in the annotated bibliography, students may write extended research papers on the various topics suggested in the book.

9. It is long enough to give a complete picture of Andrew Carnegie yet brief enough to serve as a supplement for a larger American history textbook, particularly for a teacher who wants to focus sharply on one of the personalities of this period. It should serve well the needs of teachers in an American History Survey or in advanced courses in American Social, Intellectual, and Economic History.

ACKNOWLEDGMENTS

The author is grateful to the following reviewers who read this text in manuscript form and made constructive suggestions on ways to make it more useful to teachers and students: Janet G. Brantley, Texarkana College; Tracy Campbell, University of Kentucky; Eileen Eagan, University of Southern Maine; Michael S. Mayer, University of Montana; William L. O'Neill, Rutgers University; Alice E. Reagan, Northern Virginia Community College, Woodbridge; R. B. Rosenburg, Clayton College and State University; and Donald R. Shaffer, University of Northern Colorado.

ABOUT THE AUTHOR

Dr. James T. Baker is a graduate of Baylor and Florida State Universities. He holds the title of University Distinguished Professor of History at Western Kentucky University. He has been a Fulbright Senior Lecturer in American Studies in both Korea and Taiwan, and for twenty years he directed and taught in study-abroad programs for American students in Britain and Ireland. He is now director of the United States Interns to the Canadian Parliament Program in Ottawa. He has published books on figures such as Thomas Merton, Jimmy Carter, Eric Hoffer, Ayn Rand, Brooks Hays, and Studs Terkel. Professor Baker serves as series editor for the Creators of the American Mind series and has contributed earlier volumes on Nat Turner, Eleanor Roosevelt, and Abraham Lincoln.

Time Line of Carnegie's Life

1835   Born November 25 in Dunfermline, Scotland, to Margaret Morrison and William Carnegie

1848   Moved with parents to Allegheny, Pennsylvania; began working as a bobbin-boy in a cotton processing factory for $1.20 per week

1849   Became a messenger boy for a Pittsburgh telegraph office; soon learned to take and send messages

1853   Became secretary and telegrapher for Thomas A. Scott of the Pennsylvania Railroad

1859   Named superintendent of the Pittsburgh division when Scott became vice president of the company

1861   Followed Scott to Washington and was placed in charge of all Eastern military rail and telegraphic lines for the Union Army

1865   Left Penn Rail to enter private business with his own firm, the Keystone Bridge Works

1868   Established Union Iron Mills

1873   Entered full time into the steel business, employing the new method invented by Henry Bessemer

1882   Joined forces with Henry Clay Frick and his coke company

1883   Began his career as a writer, contributing to magazines

1884   Published *Round the World*

1886   Published *Triumphant Democracy;* death of his mother

1887   Married Louise Whitfield

1889   Published "The Gospel of Wealth" as an article in the *North American Review*

1892   The Homestead Strike put down; Carnegie's break with Frick

1897   Daughter Margaret born

1899   Carnegie Steel Company controlled the bulk of U.S. steel production

1900   Published *The Gospel of Wealth*

1901   Sold steel holdings for $300,000,000; began philanthropic endeavors

1902   Established the Carnegie Institution of Washington

1906   Established the Carnegie Foundation for the Advancement of Teaching

1907   Built the Peace Palace at the World Court in The Hague

1909   Wrote autobiography, published posthumously in 1924

1910   Established the Carnegie Endowment for International Peace

1911   Established the Carnegie Corporation of New York

1913   Established the United Kingdom Trust

1919   Died August 11 at his Shadowbrook estate in Lenox, Massachusetts

Andrew Carnegie

Chapter One

THE FABULOUSLY RICH: AMERICA'S FIRST GENERATION OF MULTIMILLIONAIRES

> ". . . Lincoln saved the union and pre-
> served it . . . for no heirs more appetiz-
> ing than the proprietors of the Gilded
> Age."
>
> MURRAY KEMPTON
> *Rebellions, Perversities, and*
> *Main Events*

The United States had only a handful of millionaires before the end of the Civil War. From colonial days, there were prosperous Americans, but their wealth was in the form of land, mercantile enterprises, or both. There were only a few men like Stephen Girard, a Philadelphian born in France, who made his fortune in other enterprises, first in shipping and later in banking. Few Americans before 1865 could produce a million dollars upon demand; and in 1855 the *New York Sun* reported that the richest single American then was William B. Astor, who was estimated to be worth $6,000,000. Gun makers who supplied the armed forces during the war and Wall Street war speculators profited from the national crisis, adding to the number of men with liquid wealth. Yet even in 1865 a man worth as much as $100,000 was considered rich, and a millionaire was a rarity.

Between 1865 and 1900, however, the U.S. economy underwent an enormous change. An agrarian and mercantile nation gave way to an

urban, industrial nation; and the number of millionaires increased expo-
nentially. By 1900, although it was not common to come in contact
with them unless one lived in one of the large industrial cities of the
Northeast, millionaires were no longer rare. Moreover, there were then
many multimillionaires. The inventors and entrepreneurs who accumulated these great fortunes, this first generation of the fabulously rich,
came to be seen as heroes by many Americans. Those who had been
born poor and grown rich through their own initiative and talent were
especially admired.

In the early days of the American Republic, the archetypal
American hero was someone like George Washington or Thomas
Jefferson, men born into the landed or educated aristocracy, who out
of love for country sacrificed personal comfort and financial security to
go into battle, serve in the government, or both. Washington and
Jefferson found their personal finances in ruins after their years spent
serving the common good. In those early days, most people found it
hard to believe that a man born in poverty could become a national
leader. They would have been incredulous had they been told that
within a century America's heroes would not be military or governmental officials but entrepreneurs and financiers.

It was Andrew Jackson who helped establish a new kind of
American hero. Although by the time he became president he was a
well-to-do landowner, Jackson was born poor; had little formal education; and earned his wealth, prominence, and eventually the White
House in the election of 1828 through personal determination and
tenacity. Although Americans of the old aristocracy scorned him, he
became a hero to a younger generation who believed that they too
could rise from poverty to prominence through hard work. William
Henry Harrison, elected president in 1840, was presented to the
American people as a man born in a log cabin—despite evidence to the
contrary—in order to make the public think that he shared Jackson's
personal achievement. In 1860, candidate Abraham Lincoln truly
embodied this new hero: born in a log cabin, modestly and for the most
part self-educated, soon to recognized as be the most eloquent
spokesman for American ideals of his generation.

Lincoln was both the crowning jewel of this mid-nineteenth century heroic ideal and the last of his kind. Unlike the earlier aristocratic
statesmen, he was a politician who worked his way up from poverty to
national prominence; and unlike the entrepreneurs to come, he died
without great wealth. After the Civil War, as the Industrial Revolution
in which Carnegie made his fortune came thundering onto the scene,

a completely new kind of hero emerged. The ideal of the poor boy who made good persisted—indeed, it grew even stronger—but that boy no longer grew up to be a statesman. Responding to the material rewards of the new age of industrial opportunity, he became an inventor, an entrepreneur, a manager, a businessman, or a financier. His goal was not to serve in Congress or be president but to invent a new product, run a company, and live in a mansion far more impressive than the White House. It has been noted that the United States did not have a single "great" president (and few great statesmen of any kind) between 1865 and 1901; that is, between Abraham Lincoln and Theodore Roosevelt. Americans were busy becoming multimillionaires, and those who succeeded were admired and imitated.

Social commentator Murray Kempton's observation at the opening of this chapter locates the point at which the American image of the hero shifted from statesman to entrepreneur. Mr. Lincoln had been dead for only a short time when the Union he preserved became home to a group of men called by their admirers "captains of industry" and by their critics "robber barons." This latter term was used by Midwestern farmers to castigate railroad owners who charged them exorbitant prices to ship their products to market. It gained popular usage almost overnight and is still commonly employed to describe the new men of wealth who by 1900 had become American heroes.

These multimillionaires took advantage of opportunities that lay before them. The Industrial Revolution that had begun in England in the 1780s and spread to parts of the continent of Europe in the 1830s arrived in the United States by midcentury. Fortunes were waiting to be made in the time between the Civil War and the turn of the twentieth century; and the inventive, the industrious, the unscrupulous went for them. Federal and state governments encouraged them. Unlike Britain and the industrialized European nations, the United States had few labor unions to protect workers and few laws to prevent pollution of the environment and manipulation of stock. There were few personal or corporate taxes and no prohibitions against monopolies. Authorities regularly gave legal and even military support to the owners of factories threatened with labor action. In that day, few people considered this odd. It was the perfect milieu for "robbers" to become "barons."

Some of the new American heroes were inventors such as Thomas Alva Edison and Alexander Graham Bell, who certainly profited from their inventions but did not become as fabulously rich as other men. Some of the new fabulously rich, men like Jay Gould, Daniel Drew, and

Jim Fisk, all unscrupulous financiers, invented nothing and were little more than economic vultures. But there was also a group of men, not inventors *per se* but not merely financial manipulators either, who cornered markets and made themselves multimillionaires. Despite condemnation by labor leaders, journalists, and other reformers, they gave names and faces to the new American hero.

Among these was Cornelius Vanderbilt, known as "Commodore" because he began his rise to wealth as a sailor of sorts. Vanderbilt was born the son of a poor ferryman on Staten Island in 1794. Encouraged by an aggressive mother, unable to persuade his unambitious father to expand the family business, he formed a ferry company of his own while still a teenager. Before the age of forty he owned a fleet of steamboats. Taking advantage of opportunities offered by the California Gold Rush and the Civil War, he was by 1865 a wealthy man. Realizing that the economic future lay on land rather than on the nation's rivers, he then invested in railroads, persuading the state government in New York to give him exclusive franchises in certain profitable regions. He died in 1877 the richest man in America, leaving his son William Henry Vanderbilt a fortune of some $100,000,000. Only eight years later, with the family fortune continuing to multiply, William Henry himself died the richest man in the world. The Commodore's wealth is today visible in several luxurious "American castles"; a university in Nashville, Tennessee, named after him; and a number of rather undistinguished descendants. Yet Vanderbilt was the first of the "robber barons" to be judged and honored by the new industrial society as a hero.

John Davison Rockefeller, born in upstate New York in 1839, the son of a travelling salesman, grew up in modest if not desperate circumstances. At the end of the Civil War he was still a bookkeeper working in Cleveland, Ohio; but he foresaw one of the directions the newly dawning industrial age would take and made the most of it. In 1865 he and his brother invested $4,000 in an oil and kerosene refinery and within five years founded the company that became Standard Oil of Ohio. When investigative journalists called "muckrakers" exposed and condemned his business practices as monopolistic and harmful to the cherished free enterprise system, and when newly enacted laws threatened his enterprise, Rockefeller formed in 1881 the Standard Oil Trust, a holding company that allowed him to circumvent the new rules and continue to build his fortune. When the Ohio Supreme Court outlawed his Trust, he replaced it in 1899 with the Standard Oil Company of New Jersey, which was itself finally ordered broken up into smaller units by the U.S. Supreme Court in 1911.

Around the time of this last verdict, vociferously denying journalists' estimates that he was worth $1,000,000,000, Rockefeller turned his empire over to his son John D. Rockefeller Jr. For a decade, the senior Rockefeller had made contributions to "charitable" causes, modestly emulating the example of the steel tycoon Andrew Carnegie. In retirement, however, he sought to match and then surpass Carnegie as a conspicuous philanthropist. He richly endowed the University of Chicago and created institutes to support medical research, education, and the arts around the country. Unlike those of Carnegie, however, his contributions to various causes did not significantly reduce the fortune that he had accrued; and he died leaving his offspring the richest family in America.

In 1873 Mark Twain wrote a book called *The Gilded Age* which gave a name to the period in which robber barons flourished. Twain supposedly borrowed the phrase from a line in Shakespeare's *King John*, in which an adviser warned the king that a second coronation he was considering would be a mistake: "To gild refined gold, to paint the lily—is wasteful and ridiculous excess." Twain's term, which immediately caught on and has been used ever since, implied that the era of Vanderbilt and Rockefeller was not a golden age in American history, but was instead gilded—superficially splendid but cheap beneath the surface. The great mansions where men of enormous wealth lived were built with ill-gotten gain. Mark Twain admitted that the word "gilded" was also a play on words; there was a great deal of "guilt" about the age. Even the robber barons who became conspicuous philanthropists failed to give the men whose labor made them rich what our present society would consider proper compensation and benefits. Even contemporary critics charged that their very philanthropic enterprises were attempts to deflect attention from the way they earned their fortunes. But such doubts and warnings did little to diminish the steady growth of popular admiration for the multimillionaire as American hero.

Probably the best example of this kind of hero was Andrew Carnegie, the most prominent of the new fabulously rich Americans to have been born outside the United States. There is, in fact, some doubt that Carnegie ever became an American citizen, although he was rich enough not to be questioned about this minor detail on any of the many times he entered and left the country. Carnegie, whose fortune fell chronologically between those made by Vanderbilt and Rockefeller, was born in truly abject poverty in Scotland. He was brought to the United States by his destitute parents when he was not quite thirteen. He worked his way up from factory hand to message boy to telegrapher to railroad manager. He invested in the iron industry, then in steel, and in 1901 when he sold his assets at the age of 65 he was the richest man in the world, worth one-third of a billion dollars. Instead of keeping all his earnings as did Vanderbilt and his offspring, instead of keeping back from his charitable giving a family fortune as did Rockefeller, Carnegie began as quickly as possible to give his fortune away—at a time before there were ways to make "charity" in any way profitable. Although he lived sumptuously in his old age and left a legacy for his wife and daughter that made them far more than comfortably rich, he gave away all of the $300,000,000 he received when he sold his steel mills. His name is today associated with education, libraries, cultural centers, scientific research, and efforts to secure world peace.

As the prototypical "poor boy who made good," the example of the "rags to riches" story, Carnegie became an American ideal. As a business tycoon, a hugely successful captain of industry, and an "emperor of steel," he became an American icon. As a conspicuous philanthropist, a man who voluntarily gave most of his wealth away, he became to many people an American saint. He surpassed his predecessor Vanderbilt in fortune and certainly in philanthropy; and he surpassed his successor Rockefeller in philosophical imagination, literary articulation, and the degree of his philanthropy. Carnegie was the quintessential robber baron who was also the quintessential American hero.

Chapter Two

THE RAGS TO RICHES SUCCESS STORY: ANDREW CARNEGIE AS AMERICAN IDEAL

> "Do not be fastidious. Take what the gods offer."
>
> ANDREW CARNEGIE
> *Cornell Address, 1896*

Andrew Carnegie was born November 25, 1835, in Dunfermline, Scotland. He was the oldest child of a weaver named William Carnegie and his wife Margaret Morrison, whose family were cobblers. Queen Margaret, for whom his mother was named, is revered as Scotland's most prominent female saint. The apostle Andrew, for whom the boy was named, is said to have brought Christianity to Scotland. The family name Carnegie came from the Scots Gaelic language and was originally spelled *Caither an eige,* meaning Fort-in-the-Gap.

Dunfermline, located near the north shore of the Firth of Forth, was chosen as the first capital of a united Scotland by King Malcolm Canmore, husband of Saint Queen Margaret. There the king built a great abbey that rivaled in prestige the contemporary Abbey of Westminster in England. Medieval festivals were held there, drawing visitors from all Scotland; Robert the Bruce, greatest of Scottish heroes, was buried there as well. Carnegie was raised amid stories of great past deeds, told in the phrases and rhythms of gifted Scottish poets such as Robert Burns. He was unable to obtain much formal education, attending school briefly and sporadically, but throughout his life he read vociferously, making use of public libraries until he could afford books. His greatest interest was Scotland's rich historical and cultural heritage.

By 1835 Dunfermline had long since ceased to be Scotland's capital, eclipsed by both Glasgow and Edinburgh, and the excesses of the Calvinist Reformation had left the abbey a ruin. Dunfermline's single industry, linen weaving, was in decline. William Carnegie, who employed the common hand looms of the day, was forced to sell off all but one of his machines, and he worked it from the two-room house where he and his family lived. He was just one of millions of skilled laborers driven to economic ruin by industrialization. Andrew was born at a time of great economic despair.

In their financial plight, the Carnegies and the Morrisons became political radicals. They supported the Chartist Movement from its inception in 1838 to the day its "charter" of demands for the working classes was laughed out of Parliament in 1848. They were also anti-royal and anti-aristocracy, decrying the effects on their nation of class and privilege. Andrew Carnegie, despite becoming the richest man in the world, always considered himself a liberal, a radical, and a friend of the poor working classes, opposed to men of lordly social position. He was a walking paradox, as he also thoroughly enjoyed his own lordly social position.

The Carnegies were also religious nonconformists. The Calvinist Presbyterian Church was the legally established religion of Scotland, but they boasted that there was "not one orthodox Presbyterian in our family circle." When Andrew was a baby, his father walked out of a Church of Scotland worship service because he considered a sermon on predestination, in which the minister preached the doctrine of infant damnation, to be irrational and barbaric. For a time in Scotland William Carnegie attended Baptist services, primarily because the Baptists were free of state support and control; and after arriving in America he joined the Swedenborgian movement. This sect, formally known as the Church of the New Jerusalem, was founded in the seventeenth century by Emmanuel Swedenborg, a Swedish scientist and author; and it appealed to a man of William's pious-rationalist bent. Andrew's mother showed little interest in formal religion and in fact saw to it that Andrew was exempted from religious studies in the school he attended for a brief time in Dunfermline.

As a boy in America, Andrew attended Swedenborgian services with his father but never became a member of the congregation. At the time of his death he was still not a member of any church. Yet despite his own claims of freedom from religious influences, especially "Presbyterian" ones, Carnegie's biographers have noted that he

Brown Brothers, Sterling, PA.

The weaver's cottage in Dunfermline, Scotland, where Carnegie was born. It is now a museum.

demonstrated many "Calvinist" traits. For him ethical behavior was a simple matter of choosing right over wrong, good over bad, a characteristic that Calvinist Puritans have exhibited the world over. Even more Calvinistic was his absolute certainty that he always chose the right and the good; that all of his causes were righteous ones; and that he was always on the side of truth and goodness.

CARNEGIE'S RISE TO THE TOP

The Carnegies finally decided in 1848—the fateful year that Parliament rejected the Charter—to abandon Scotland. On May 17 they left for America. Relatives who had gone before them helped them make their way across the Atlantic and overland to the industrial city of Pittsburgh in Pennsylvania. As Andrew approached his thirteenth birthday his family settled in the working class suburb of Allegheny. Andrew's schooling, which had been at best sketchy, ended then. He went to work full-time as a bobbin boy in a factory at a salary of $1.20 a week. Soon he was "promoted" to a job that paid $1.65 a week, but it required that he work with an oil that made him sick. Finally escaping to the healthier outdoors, he next became a telegraph delivery boy at a salary of $2.50 a week. Through all of these early days of struggle he impressed everyone around him with his determination to "get ahead."

Dissatisfied with the skimpy education he had received in Scotland, he set out to educate himself through reading. A local resident, Colonel James Anderson, opened his personal library of four hundred "well-worn books" to the "working boys" of Pittsburgh; and Carnegie became one of its most persistent visitors. He later said that it was Colonel Anderson's gift of a free library to the working poor that inspired his own decision to endow libraries across the nation. In fact, when he dedicated the Carnegie Library in Allegheny nearly half a century later, he erected a commemorative plaque to James Anderson, acknowledging his debt to the colonel.

During the time he spent at the telegraph office waiting for messages to deliver, he learned Morse Code "by sound" and became so adept at reading it that at age sixteen he was promoted to the job of telegrapher at $25.00 a month. With his father unable to make any progress in the new country (William Carnegie died in 1850, "a failure" by most reckoning, although Andrew never made mention of it), Andrew's income had to support the entire family. In 1853, at age eighteen, due in large part to his reputation for zealous dedication to hard work, he was chosen to be personal assistant to Thomas Scott, western regional superintendent of the Pennsylvania Railroad, and was credited with helping Scott take advantage of a period of rapid railroad expansion to enlarge the corporation's services and earnings.

When Scott was made vice president of Penn Rail, he showed his appreciation for Carnegie's support by appointing him to his old post as superintendent of the western division. At the outbreak of the Civil War in 1861, Scott took Carnegie to Washington to help him organize rail communications in the Union states; and only when that task was completed did Carnegie return to Pittsburgh to supervise the vital western Pennsylvania link through the remaining years of the war. There he worked until the war ended in 1865.

Even during the war years, however, as he performed what he considered his patriotic duties to his adopted country by helping to keep supplies moving by rail, Carnegie began investing in various other enterprises. In 1856 he began his career as a "capitalist" by purchasing ten shares of Adams Express Company at fifty dollars a share, with money his mother raised by mortgaging the small house the family had been able to buy. Then T. T. Woodruff presented him with a plan to build sleeping cars for rail passengers, and Carnegie sold the idea to Scott and Penn Rail. He himself bought stock in the Woodruff Sleeping Car Company with $217 borrowed from a friendly banker. From both

Carnegie House on Fifth Avenue, New York.

investments he almost immediately made handsome profits, and it was not long before he recognized that he had a knack for accumulating wealth. By 1863 his yearly income was around $45,000, only $2,400 of which came from his job with the railroad.

In 1865 he left Penn Rail to devote himself full time to his investments, most of which now involved the use of iron, so plentiful in western Pennsylvania. In partnership with his younger brother Thomas and several childhood friends, he founded the Keystone Bridge Company, first building iron bridges and then providing iron rails for the rapidly expanding national system of railroads. He profited from the post-war economic boom that enriched the states which had been loyal to the Union. In 1867 he and his widowed mother moved from Pittsburgh, where most of his manufacturing continued to be done, to the St. Nicholas Hotel in New York City, where the money he needed to expand his empire could be raised. In 1868, at age 33, he was worth $400,000. He found that raising, investing, and multiplying money gave him great pleasure and fulfillment. He was more than once seen rubbing his hands and laughing gleefully as he confided to friends, "I'm rich, I'm rich."

He had come a long way in twenty years from the ragged son of destitute immigrants who despised people of high economic and social standing. At 33 he was as rich and famous as any of those people the Carnegies hated. Yet the story of his rise to fabulous wealth, international fame, and social and cultural influence was just beginning. He was already an American success story, but it was at that time impossible to foresee that when he retired at age 65 he would be worth well over a third of a billion dollars.

CARNEGIE'S ACCOUNT OF HOW HE SUCCEEDED

Carnegie the financier always longed to be Carnegie the intellectual. Throughout his life he was a disciplined, vigorous reader; and after his fiftieth birthday, when he had time to indulge his deepest longings, he began to write articles, then books. He also took advantage of invitations to address all kinds of audiences. It is therefore possible, by consulting the large collection of his published musings, to know how Carnegie saw himself and how he wanted others to see him, how he believed and wanted his readers to believe he rose from rags to riches. His speeches and writing were propaganda, to be sure, but even as such they provide insight into Carnegie's mind, even as he spun his own tale.

He was convinced, he said, that early poverty actually helped him succeed. In a lecture at Union College in Schenectady, New York, in January 1895, he told his audience," . . . I heartily subscribe to President Garfield's doctrine, that 'The richest heritage a young man can be born to is poverty.' I make no idle prediction when I say that it is from that class [the poor] from whom the good and the great will spring. It is not from the sons of the millionaire or the noble that the world receives its teachers, its martyrs, its inventors, its statesmen, its poets, or even its men of affairs. It is from the cottage of the poor that all these spring." (This appears in Carnegie's *Empire of Business,* "Wealth and Its Uses," p. 105. See the annotated bibliography in Chapter 7.) He made this point again in the following article, "How I Served My Apprenticeship," which appeared in *Youth's Companion*, on April 23, 1896.

> On arriving in Allegheny City . . . my father entered a cotton factory. I soon followed, and served as a "bobbin-boy," and this is how I began my preparation for subsequent apprenticeship as a business man. I received one dollar and twenty cents a week, and was then just about twelve years old.
>
> I cannot tell you how proud I was when I received my first week's own earnings. One dollar and twenty cents made by myself

and given to me because I had been of some use in the world! No longer entirely dependent upon my parents, but at last admitted to the family partnership as a contributing member and able to help them! I think this makes a man out of a boy sooner than almost anything else, and a real man, too, if there be any germ of true manhood in him. It is everything to feel that you are useful.

I have had to deal with great sums. Many millions of dollars have since passed through my hands. But the genuine satisfaction I had from that one dollar and twenty cents outweighs any subsequent pleasure in money-getting. It was the direct reward of honest, manual labor; it represented a week of very hard work—so hard that, but for the aim and end which sanctified it, slavery might not be much too strong a term to describe it.

For a lad of twelve to rise and breakfast every morning, except the blessed Sunday morning, and go into the streets and find his way to the factory and begin to work while it was still dark outside, and not be released until after darkness came again in the evening, forty minutes' interval only being allowed at noon, was a terrible task.

But I was young and had my dreams, and something within always told me that this would not, could not, should not last—I should some day get into a better position. Besides this, I felt myself no longer a mere boy, but quite a little man, and this made me happy.

A change soon came, for a kind old Scotsman, who knew some of our relatives, made bobbins, and took me into his factory before I was thirteen. But here for a time it was even worse than in the cotton factory, because I was set to fire a boiler in the cellar, and actually to run the small steam engine which drove the machinery. The firing of the boiler was all right, for fortunately we did not use coal, but the refuse wooden chips; and I always liked to work in wood. But the responsibility of keeping the water right and of running the engine, and the danger of my making a mistake and blowing the whole factory to pieces, caused too great a strain, and I often awoke and found myself sitting up in bed through the night, trying the steam-gauges. But I never told them at home that I was having a hard tussle. No, no! everything must be bright to them.

This was a point of honor, for every member of the family was working hard, except, of course, my little brother, who was then a child, and we were telling each other only all the bright things. Besides this, no man would whine and give up—he would die first.

There was no servant in our family, and several dollars per week were earned by the mother by binding shoes after her daily work was done! Father was also hard at work in the factory. And could I complain?

My kind employer, John Hay,—peace to his ashes!—soon relieved me of the undue strain, for he needed some one to make out bills and keep his accounts, and finding that I could write a

plain school-boy hand and could "cipher," he made me his only
clerk. But still I had to work hard upstairs in the factory, for the
clerking took but little time.

You know how people moan about poverty as being a great evil,
and it seems to be accepted that if people had only plenty of money
and were rich, they would be happy and more useful, and get more
out of life.

As a rule, there is more genuine satisfaction, a truer life, and more
obtained from life in the humble cottages of the poor than in the
palaces of the rich. I always pity the sons and daughters of rich
men, who are attended by servants, and have governesses at a later
age, but am glad to remember that they do not know what they
have missed.

They have kind fathers and mothers, too, and think that they
enjoy the sweetness of these blessings to the fullest: but this they
cannot do; for the poor boy who has in his father his constant companion, tutor, and model, and in his mother—holy name!—his nurse,
teacher, guardian angel, saint, all in one, has a richer, more precious
fortune in life than any rich man's son who is not so favored can
possibly know, and compared with which all other fortunes count
for little.

It is because I know how sweet and happy and pure the home
of honest poverty is, how free from perplexing care, from social
envies and emulations, how loving and how united its members
may be in the common interest of supporting the family, that I sympathize with the rich man's boy and congratulate the poor man's
boy; and it is for these reasons that from the ranks of the poor so
many strong, eminent, self-reliant men have always sprung and
always must spring.

If you will read the list of the immortals who "were not born to
die," you will find that most of them have been born to the precious
heritage of poverty.

It seems, nowadays, a matter of universal desire that poverty
should be abolished. We should be quite willing to abolish luxury,
but to abolish honest, industrious, self-denying poverty would be
to destroy the soil upon which mankind produces the virtues
which enable our race to reach a still higher civilization than it
now possesses.

I come now to the third step in my apprenticeship, for I had
already taken two, as you see—the cotton factory and then the bobbin factory; and with the third—the third time is the chance, you
know—deliverance came. I obtained a situation as messenger boy
in the telegraph office of Pittsburg when I was fourteen. Here I
entered a new world.

Amid books, newspapers, pencils, pens and ink and writing-pads, and a clean office, bright windows, and the literary atmosphere, I was the happiest boy alive.

My only dread was that I should some day be dismissed because I did not know the city; for it is necessary that a messenger boy should know all the firms and addresses of men who are in the habit of receiving telegrams. But I was a stranger in Pittsburg. However, I made up my mind that I would learn to repeat successively each business house in the principal streets, and was soon able to shut my eyes and begin at one side of Wood Street, and call every firm successively to the top, then pass to the other side and call every firm to the bottom. Before long I was able to do this with the business streets generally. My mind was then at rest upon that point.

Of course every messenger boy wants to become an operator, and before the operators arrive[d] in the early mornings the boys slipped up to the instruments and practised. This I did, and was soon able to talk to the boys in the other offices along the line, who were also practising.

One morning I heard Philadelphia calling Pittsburg and giving the signal, "Death message." Great attention was then paid to "death messages," and I thought I ought to try to take this one. I answered and did so, and went off and delivered it before the operator came. After that the operators sometimes used to ask me to work for them.

Having a sensitive ear for sound, I soon learned to take messages by the ear, which was then very uncommon—I think only two persons in the United States could then do it. Now every operator takes by ear, so easy it is to follow and do what any other boy can— if you only have to. This brought me into notice, and finally I became an operator, and received the, to me, enormous recompense of twenty-five dollars per month—three hundred dollars a year!

This was a fortune—the very sum I had fixed when I was a factory-worker as the fortune I wished to possess, because the family could live on three hundred dollars a year and be almost or quite independent. Here it was at last! But I was soon to be in receipt of extra compensation for extra work.

The six newspapers of Pittsburg received telegraphic news in common. Six copies of each dispatch were made by a gentleman who received six dollars per week for the work, and he offered me a gold dollar per week if I would do it, of which I was very glad indeed, because I always liked to work with news and scribble for newspapers.

The reporter came to a room every evening for the news which I had prepared, and this brought me into most pleasant intercourse with these clever fellows, and besides, I got a dollar a week as pocket-money, for this was not considered family revenue by me.

I think this last step of doing something beyond one's task is fully entitled to be considered "business." The other revenue, you see, was just salary obtained for regular work; but here was a little business operation upon my own account, and I was proud indeed of my gold dollar every week.

The Pennsylvania Railroad shortly after this was completed to Pittsburg, and that genius, Thomas A Scott, was its superintendent. He often came to the telegraph office to talk to his chief, the general superintendent, at Altoona, and I became known to him in this way.

When that great railway system put up a wire of its own, he asked me to be his clerk and operator; so I left the telegraph office—in which there is great danger that a young man may be permanently buried, as it were—and became connected with the railways.

The new appointment was accompanied by what was, to me, a tremendous increase of salary. It jumped from twenty-five to thirty-five dollars per month. Mr. Scott was then receiving one hundred and twenty-five dollars per month, and I used to wonder what on earth he could do with so much money.

I remained for thirteen years in the services of Pennsylvania Railroad Company, and was at last superintendent of the Pittsburg division of the road, successor to Mr. Scott, who had in the meantime risen to the office of vice-president of the company.

One day Mr. Scott, who was the kindest of men, and had taken a great fancy to me, asked if I had or could find five hundred dollars to invest.

Here the business instinct came into play. I felt that as the door was opened for a business investment with my chief, it would be wilful flying in the face of providence if I did not jump at it; so I answered promptly:

"Yes sir; I think I can."

"Very well," he said, "get it; a man has just died who owns ten shares in the Adams Express Company which I want you to buy. It will cost you fifty dollars per share, and I can help you with a little balance if you cannot raise it all."

Here was a queer position. The available assets of the whole family were not five hundred dollars. But there was one member of the family whose ability, pluck, and resource never failed us, and I felt sure the money could be raised somehow or other by my mother.

Indeed, had Mr. Scott known our position he would have advanced it himself; but the last thing in the world the proud Scot will do is to reveal his poverty and rely upon others. The family had managed by this time to purchase a small house and pay for it in order to save rent. My recollection is that it was worth eight hundred dollars.

The matter was laid before the council of three that night, and the oracle spoke: "Must be done. Mortgage our house. I will take the steamer in the morning for Ohio, and see uncle, and ask him to arrange it. I am sure he can." This was done. Of course her visit was successful—where did she ever fail?

The money was procured, paid over; ten shares of Adams Express Company stock was mine; but no one knew our little home had been mortgaged "to give our boy a start."

Adams Express stock then paid monthly dividends of one per cent, and the first check for five dollars arrived. I can see it now, and I well remember the signature of "J.C. Babcock, Cashier," who wrote a big "John Hancock" hand.

The next day being Sunday, we boys—myself and my ever-constant companions—took our usual Sunday afternoon stroll in the country, and sitting down in the woods, I showed them this check, saying, "Eureka! We have found it."

Here was something new to all of us, for none of us had ever received anything but from our toil. A return from capital was something strange and new.

How money could make money, how, without any attention from me, this mysterious golden visitor should come, led to much speculation upon the part of the young fellows, and I was for the first time hailed as a "capitalist."

You see, I was beginning to serve my apprenticeship as a business man in a satisfactory manner.

A very important incident in my life occurred when, one day in a train, a nice, farmer looking gentleman approached me, saying that the conductor had told him I was connected with the Pennsylvania Railroad, and he would like to show me something. He pulled from a small green bag the model of the first sleeping-car. This was Mr. Woodruff, the inventor.

Its value struck me like a flash. I asked him to come to Altoona the following week, and he did so. Mr. Scott, with his usual quickness, grasped the idea. A contract was made with Mr. Woodruff to put two trial cars on the Pennsylvania Railroad. Before leaving Altoona Mr. Woodruff came and offered me an interest in the venture, which I promptly accepted. But how I was to make my payments rather troubled me, for the cars were to be paid for in monthly installments after delivery, and my first monthly payment was to be two hundred and seventeen dollars and a half.

I had not the money, and I did not see any way of getting it. But I finally decided to visit the local banker and ask him for a loan, pledging myself to repay at the rate of fifteen dollars per month. He promptly granted it. Never shall I forget his putting his arm over my shoulder, saying, "Oh, yes, Andy; you are all right!"

I then and there signed my first note. Proud day this; and surely now no one will dispute that I was becoming a "business man." I had signed my first note, and, most important of all,—for any fellow can sign a note,—I had found a banker willing to take it as "good."

My subsequent payments were made by the receipts from the sleeping-cars, and I really made my first considerable sum from this investment in the Woodruff Sleeping-car Company, which was afterward absorbed by Mr. Pullman—a remarkable man whose name is now known over all the world.

Shortly after this I was appointed superintendent of the Pittsburg division, and returned to my dear old home, smoky Pittsburg. Wooden bridges were then used exclusively upon the rail-ways, and the Pennsylvania Railroad was experimenting with a bridge built of cast-iron. I saw that wooden bridges would not do for the future, and organized a company in Pittsburg to build iron bridges.

Here again I had recourse to the bank, because my share of the capital was twelve hundred and fifty dollars, and I had not the money; but the bank lent it to me, and we began the Keystone Bridge Works, which proved a great success. This company built the first great bridge over the Ohio River, three hundred feet span, and has built many of the most important structures since.

This was my beginning in manufacturing; and from that start all our other works have grown, the profits of one building the other. My "apprenticeship" as a business man soon ended, for I resigned my position as an officer of the Pennsylvania Railroad Company to give exclusive attention to business.

I was no longer merely an official working for others upon a salary, but a full-fledged business man working upon my own account.

I never was quite reconciled to working for other people. At the most, the railway officer has to look forward to the enjoyment of a stated salary, and he has a great many people to please; even if he gets to be president, he has sometimes a board of directors who cannot know what is best to be done; and even if this board be satisfied, he has a board of stockholders to criticize him, and as the property is not his own he cannot manage it as he pleases.

I always liked the idea of being my own master, of manufacturing something and giving employment to many men. There is only one thing to think of manufacturing if you are a Pittsburger, for Pittsburg even then had asserted her supremacy as the "Iron City," the leading iron-and-steel-manufacturing city in America.

So my indispensable and clever partners, who had been my boy companions, I am delighted to say,—some of the very boys who had met in the grove to wonder at the five-dollar check,—began business, and still continue extending it to meet the ever-growing and ever-changing wants of our most progressive country, year after year.

Always we are hoping that we need expand no farther; yet ever we are finding that to stop expanding would be to fall behind; and even to-day the successive improvements and inventions follow each other so rapidly that we see just as much yet to be done as ever.

When the manufacturer of steel ceases to grow he begins to decay, so we must keep on extending. The result of all these developments is that three pounds of finished steel are now bought in Pittsburg for two cents, which is cheaper than anywhere else on the earth, and that our country has become the greatest producer of iron in the world.

And so ends the story of my apprenticeship and graduation as a business man.

Perhaps it was his pride in overcoming early poverty that made Carnegie insensitive to the struggles of the poor men who worked for him, men who had not advanced. Yet he admitted that in his early days he found the life of the very workers whose labor made him rich, to whom he gave so few benefits in order to increase his own profits, boring and destructive. He did not speculate on the kind of life he would have lived had he not been offered a rope to climb out of the deep pit of daily physical labor. He also ignored the logical conclusion of his argument: that if all men escaped labor and became great financiers the way he did, they would rob their own children of the wonderful privilege of growing up poor.

Carnegie thought he had benefited by starting at the bottom of the corporate ladder and working his way up. He loved to advise young men on how to become successful businessmen; and in the following rather avuncular address to a group of business college men in 1885, he strongly emphasized the need to rise through the ranks. It was at the bottom that the real lessons of success were learned.

It is well that young men should begin at the beginning and occupy the most subordinate positions. Many of the leading business men of Pittsburgh had a serious responsibility thrust upon them at the very threshold of their career. They were introduced to the broom, and spent the first hours of their business lives sweeping out the office. I notice we have janitors and janitresses now in offices, and our young men unfortunately miss that salutary branch of a business education. But if by chance the professional sweeper is absent any morning the boy who has the genius of the future partner in him will not hesitate to try his hand at the broom. The other day a fond fashionable mother in Michigan asked a young man whether he had

ever seen a young lady sweep in a room so grandly as her Priscilla.
He said no, he never had, and the mother was gratified beyond
measure, but then said he, after a pause, "What I should like to see
her do is sweep out a room." It does not hurt the newest comer to
sweep out the office if necessary. I was one of those sweepers
myself, and who do you suppose were my fellow sweepers? David
McCargo, now superintendent of the Allegheny Valley Railroad;
Robert Pitcairn, Superintendent of the Pennsylvania Railroad, and
Mr. Moreland, City Attorney. We all took turns, two each morning did
the sweeping; and now I remember Davie was so proud of his clean
white shirt bosom that he used to spread over it an old silk bandana
handkerchief which he kept for the purpose, and we other boys
thought he was putting on airs. So he was. None of us had a silk
handkerchief.

Assuming that you have all obtained employment and are fairly
started, my advice to you is "aim high." I would not give a fig for the
young man who does not already see himself the partner or the
head of an important firm. Do not rest content for a moment in
your thoughts as head clerk, or foreman, or general manager in any
concern, no matter how extensive. Say each to yourself: "My place is
at the top." *Be king in your dreams.* Make your vow that you will
reach that position, with untarnished reputation, and make no other
vow to distract your attention, except the very commendable one
that when you are a member of the firm or before that, if you have
been promoted two or three times, you will form another partnership with the loveliest of her sex—a partnership to which our new
partnership act has no application. The liability there is limited . . .

I can give you the secret. It lies mainly in this. Instead of the question, "What must I do for my employer?" substitute "What can I do?"
Faithful and conscientious discharge of the duties assigned you is all
very well, but the verdict in such cases generally is that you perform
your present duties so well that you had better continue performing
them. Now, young gentlemen, this will not do. It will not do for the
coming partners. There must be something beyond this. We make
Clerks, Bookkeepers, Treasurers, Bank Tellers of this class, and there
they remain to the end of the chapter. The rising man must do something exceptional, and beyond the range of his special department.
He must attract attention. A shipping clerk, he may do so by discovering in an invoice an error with which he has nothing to do, and
which has escaped the attention of the proper party. If a weighing
clerk, he may save for the firm by doubting the adjustment of the
scales and having them corrected, even if this be the province of the
master mechanic. If a messenger boy, even he can lay the seed of
promotion by going beyond the letter of his instructions in order to

secure the desired reply. There is no service so low and simple, neither any so high, in which the young man of ability and willing disposition cannot readily and almost daily prove himself capable of greater trust and usefulness, and, what is equally important, show his invincible determination to rise. Some day, in your own department, you will be directed to do or say something which you know will prove disadvantageous to the interest of the firm. Here is your chance. Stand up like a man and say so. Say it boldly, and give your reasons, and thus prove to your employer that, while his thoughts have been engaged upon other matters, you have been studying during hours when perhaps he thought you asleep, how to advance his interests. You may be right or you may be wrong, but in either case you have gained the first condition of success. You have attracted attention. Your employer has found that he has not a mere hireling in his service, but a man; not one who is content to give so many hours a week for so many dollars in return, but one who devotes his spare hours and constant thought to the business. Such an employee must perforce be thought of, and thought of kindly and well. It will not be long before his advice is asked in his special branch, and if the advice given be sound, it will soon be asked and taken upon questions of broader bearing. This means partnership; if not with present employers then with others. Your foot, in such a case, is upon the ladder; the amount of climbing done depends entirely upon yourself . . .

There is one sure mark of the coming partner, the future millionaire; his revenues always exceed his expenditures. He begins to save early, almost as soon as he begins to earn. No matter how little it may be possible to save, save that little. Invest it securely, not necessarily in bonds, but in anything which you have good reason to believe will be profitable, but no gambling with it, remember. A rare chance will soon present itself for investment. The little you have saved will prove the basis for an amount of credit utterly surprising to you. Capitalists trust the saving young man. For every hundred dollars you can produce as the result of hard-won savings, Midas, in search of a partner, will lend or credit a thousand; for every thousand, fifty thousand. It is not capital that your seniors require, it is the man who has proved that he has the business habits which create capital, and to create it in the best of all possible ways, as far as self-discipline is concerned, is, by adjusting his habits to his means. Gentlemen, it is the first hundred dollars saved which tells. Begin at once to lay up something. The bee predominates in the future millionaire.

Thus spoke the Carnegie who rose from rags to riches. He was certain he had earned every penny of his great wealth. He was living the American dream.

CARNEGIE'S RISE IN THE AMERICAN POPULAR IMAGINATION

By rising from grinding poverty to great wealth, by doing so earlier in his life than any of the other industrialists of his age, and by remaining in the public eye for so long, Andrew Carnegie personified the American myth of the poor boy who made good. It mattered little that having been born abroad he was ineligible to be president, or that he never served his country in any elective or even appointive public office. As noted earlier, his was an age when heroes were not statesmen but industrialists. While the rags to riches myth was well established before America ever heard of Andrew Carnegie, while other men obviously contributed to the myth, and while he was not always mentioned by name in the popular stories about the new world's opportunity for the poor boy to get rich, the life of Andrew Carnegie proved the myth true for many Americans. He confirmed popular faith in the American dream. He was the late nineteenth century's American hero.

POOR BOY MAKES GOOD: A STORY BY HORATIO ALGER

No writer captured this dream and portrayed this type of hero better and more repeatedly than Horatio Alger. Born the son of a Unitarian minister in Revere, Massachusetts, in 1832, Alger failed his physical examination for the Civil War, worked for a time as a newspaper reporter, and eventually became a minister himself. While still a young man, Alger recognized the significance of the new American "age of opportunity" and turned it to good literary use. Instead of writing biographies of the poor boys who were making fortunes, accounts in which honesty might have required him to mention their personal and professional flaws, he chose to write fictional accounts of their successes, stories that portrayed them in true-blue colors.

There were over a hundred "Horatio Alger" books, mostly set in New York City, written two or three a year, all of them best-sellers in their day. In each of them, a boy rose from modest status, sometimes even abject poverty, to worldly comfort and renown, in some cases to vast fortune and fame. Each boy accomplished his goals through hard work, high personal and professional morals, a bit of luck, and a flair for righteous action at the right moment.

While Alger's early stories were written before Carnegie was widely known in the East, they clearly reflected the mythology of a nation that believed in and encouraged the rise of its Carnegies and Rockefellers. By 1875 Carnegie *was* well-known to Alger's New York, openly confirming and reinforcing this mythology, even influencing Alger's choice of names. In an 1894 story an "Irish" Andy Burke was the hero; in 1902 there was Andy Grant. Characters named Andy Gordon and Ben Bruce, both decidedly Scots and Scots-Irish in name and character, were also protagonists.

In spite of Alger's stilted prose, the fact that all of his stories had the same basic plot, and the simplistic morality they reflected, his books were tremendously popular in the age of Andrew Carnegie. Americans in the Gilded Age saw living proof of his verities in the Carnegies of the day; they wanted to believe that every boy could get rich. Many of Alger's readers doubtless agreed with Episcopal bishop of Massachusetts William Lawrence, who said, "In the long run, it is only to the man of morality that wealth comes. . . . Material prosperity is helping to make the national character sweeter, more joyous, more unselfish, more Christlike. . . . Godliness is in league with riches." (Quoted by Henry Steele Commager, *The American Mind,* pp. 53, 231.)

The following excerpt is taken from Alger's novel *Ragged Dick or Street Life in New York with the Bootblacks,* published in 1868, the year Carnegie's iron works began to pay off and he netted $50,000 income. It is the story of Richard Hunter, a poor street boy and an orphan, who made ends meet by shining boots. Although he had every sociological reason to become a petty criminal, he worked hard, saved his money, and was absolutely honest and moral. He even found a tutor (Henry Fosdick) to teach him reading, writing, and arithmetic; and he began to look for a way up the business ladder, hoping to use his rudimentary literacy to become a clerk. In other words, he was a young Andrew Carnegie, except for one detail: he had no doting, angelic mother to steer him right and raise money for any business schemes he might be offered. For 248 pages, Alger extolled the virtues of this poor boy, and near the end of the book Dick's hard work, honesty, and attempts at self-improvement paid off. "This is the way it happened," Alger began.

> As Dick had a balance of more than a hundred dollars in the savings bank, might fairly consider himself a young man of property, he thought himself justified in occasionally taking a half holiday from business, and going on an excursion. On Wednesday afternoon Henry Fosdick was sent by his employer on an errand to that part of Brooklyn near Greenwood Cemetery. Dick hastily dressed himself in his best, and determined to accompany him.
>
> The two boys walked down to the South Ferry, and, paying their two cents each, entered the ferry-boat. They remained at the stern, and stood by the railing, watching the great city, with its crowded wharves, receding from view. Beside them was a gentleman with

two children,—a girl of eight and a little boy of six. The children were talking gayly to their father. While he was pointing out some object of interest to the little girl, the boy managed to creep, unobserved, beneath the chain that extends across the boat, for the protection of passengers, and, stepping incautiously to the edge of the boat, fell over into the foaming water.

At the child's scream, the father looked up, and, with a cry of horror, sprang to the edge of the boat. He would have plunged in, but, being unable to swim, would only have endangered his own life, without being able to save his child.

"My child!" he exclaimed in anguish,—"who will save my child? A thousand—ten thousand dollars to any one who will save him!"

There chanced to be but few passengers on board at the time, and nearly all these were either in the cabins or standing forward. Among the few who saw the child fall was our hero.

Now Dick was an expert swimmer. It was an accomplishment which he had possessed for years, and he no sooner saw the boy fall than he resolved to rescue him. His determination was formed before he heard the liberal offer made by the boy's father. Indeed, I must do Dick the justice to say that, in the excitement of the moment, he did not hear it at all, nor would it have stimulated the alacrity with which he sprang to the rescue of the little boy.

Little Johnny had already risen once, and gone under for the second time, when our hero plunged in. He was obliged to strike out for the boy, and this took time. He reached him none too soon. Just as he was sinking for the third and last time, he caught him by the jacket. Dick was stout and strong, but Johnny clung to him so tightly, that it was with great difficulty he was able to sustain himself.

"Put your arms round my neck," said Dick.

The little boy mechanically obeyed, and clung with a grasp strengthened by his terror. In this position Dick could bear his weight better. But the ferry-boat was receding fast. It was quite impossible to reach it. The father, his face pale with terror and anguish, and his hands clasped in suspense, saw the brave boy's struggles, and prayed with agonizing fervor that he might be successful. But it is probable, for they were now midway of the river, that both Dick and the little boy whom he had bravely undertaken to rescue would have been drowned, had not a row-boat been fortunately near. The two men who were in it witnessed the accident, and hastened to the rescue of our hero.

"Keep up a little longer," they shouted, bending to their oars, "and we will save you."

Dick heard the shout, and it put fresh strength into him. He battled manfully with the treacherous sea, his eyes fixed longingly upon the approaching boat.

"Hold on tight, little boy," he said. "There's a boat coming."

The little boy did not see the boat. His eyes were closed to shut out the fearful water, but he clung the closer to his young preserver. Six long, steady strokes, and the boat dashed along side. Strong hands seized Dick and his youthful burden, and drew them into the boat, both dripping with water.

"God be thanked!" exclaimed the father, as from the steamer he saw the child's rescue.

"That brave little boy shall be rewarded, if I sacrifice my whole fortune to compass it."

"You've had a pretty narrow escape, young chap," said one of the boatmen to Dick. "It was a pretty tough job you undertook."

"Yes," said Dick. "That's what I thought when I was in the water. If it hadn't been for you, I don't know what would have 'come of us."

"Anyhow you're a plucky boy, or you wouldn't have dared to jump into the water after this little chap. It was a risky thing to do."

"I'm used to the water," said Dick, modestly. "I didn't stop to think of the danger, but I wasn't going to see that little fellow drown without tryin' to save him."

The boat at once headed for the ferry wharf on the Brooklyn side. The captain of the ferry-boat, seeing the rescue, did not think it necessary to stop his boat, but kept on his way. The whole occurrence took place in less time than I have occupied in telling it.

The father was waiting on the wharf to receive his little boy, with what feelings of gratitude and joy can be easily understood. With a burst of happy tears he clasped him to his arms. Dick was about to withdraw modestly, but the gentleman perceived the movement, and, putting down the child, came forward, and, clasping his hand, said with emotion, "My brave boy, I owe you a debt I can never repay. But for your timely service I should now be plunged into an anguish which I cannot think of without a shudder."

Our hero was ready enough to speak on most occasions, but always felt awkward when he was praised.

"It wasn't any trouble," he said modestly. "I can swim like a top."

"But not many boys would have risked their lives for a stranger," said the gentleman.

Dick was taken to a house nearby, warmed up, and put to bed. When he woke, he was presented with a new suit of clothes and told to come to the office of Mr. James Rockwell. At eleven the next morning he presented himself at the office, and the little boy's father rose from his desk to shake Dick's hand.

"My young friend," he said, "you have done me so great service that I wish to be of some service to you in return. Tell me about yourself, and what plans or wishes you have formed for the future."

Dick frankly related his past history, and told Mr. Rockwell of his desire to get into a store or counting-room, and of the failure of all his applications thus far. The merchant listened attentively to Dick's statement, and, when he had finished, placed a sheet of paper before him, and, handing him a pen, said, "Will you write your name on this piece of paper?"

Dick wrote in a free, bold hand, the name Richard Hunter. He had very much improved in his penmanship, as has already been mentioned, and now had no cause to be ashamed of it.

Mr. Rockwell surveyed it approvingly.

"How would you like to enter my counting-room as clerk, Richard?" he asked.

Dick was about to say "Bully," when he recollected himself, and answered, "Very much."

"I suppose you know something of arithmetic, do you not?"

"Yes, sir."

"Then you may consider yourself engaged at a salary of ten dollars a week. You may come next Monday morning."

"Ten dollars!" repeated Dick, thinking he must have misunderstood.

"Yes; will that be sufficient?"

"It's more than I can earn," said Dick, honestly.

"Perhaps it is at first," said Mr. Rockwell, smiling; "but I am willing to pay you that. I will besides advance you as fast as your progress will justify it."

Dick was so elated that he hardly restrained himself from some demonstration which would have astonished the merchant; but he exercised self-control, and only said, "I'll try to serve you so faithfully, sir, that you won't repent having taken me into your service."

"And I think you will succeed," said Mr. Rockwell, encouragingly. "I will not detain you any longer, for I have some important business to attend to. I shall expect to see you on Monday morning."

———

. . . That evening Dick and Fosdick had a long conversation. Fosdick rejoiced heartily in his friend's success, and on his side had the pleasant news to communicate that his pay had been advanced to six dollars a week.

"I think we can afford to leave Mott Street now," he continued. "This house isn't as neat as it might be, and I should like to live in a nicer quarter of the city."

"All right," said Dick. "We'll hunt up a new room to-morrow. I shall have plenty of time, having retired from business. I'll try to get

my reg'lar customers to take Johnny Nolan in my place. That boy
hasn't any enterprise. He needs somebody to look out for him."

"You might give him you box and brush, too, Dick."

"No," said Dick; "I'll give him some new ones, but mine I want to
keep, to remind me of the hard times I've had, when I was an ignorant boot-black, and never expected to be anything better."

"When, in short, you were 'Ragged Dick.' You must drop that
name, and think of yourself now as—"

"Richard Hunter, Esq.," said our hero, smiling.

"A young gentleman on the way to fame and fortune," added
Fosdick.

Here ends the story of Ragged Dick. As Fosdick said, he is Ragged
Dick no longer. He has taken a step upward, and is determined to
mount still higher. There are fresh adventures in store for him, and
for others who have been introduced in these pages. Those who
have felt interested in his early life will find his history continued in
a new volume, forming the second of the series, to be called,—

FAME AND FORTUNE;

OR

THE PROGRESS OF RICHARD HUNTER

In that next volume, published later the same year, Dick did gain
fame and fortune—by means of his continuing honesty, morality, and
hard work. In a third book, published in 1869, entitled *Mark the Match
Boy or Richard Hunter's Ward,* he did help another poor, deserving
boy like himself rise from the slums to success.

RUSSEL CONWELL'S "ACRES OF DIAMONDS"

A second writer, also a minister, who captured the optimistic air of the
age that admired and produced Carnegie-like heroes, was Russell
Conwell (1843–1925). Under Conwell's leadership, the Grace Baptist
Church of Philadelphia built its famous Temple sanctuary and became
one of the nation's largest and most influential churches. Conwell also
built a hospital and founded and served as president of the Temple's
preacher-training college, which after several metamorphoses eventually became Temple University. Having served as a captain in the Civil
War, Conwell first gave his famous sermonic address "Acres of
Diamonds" to a reunion of his old brigade in 1873, and it proved so
enduringly popular that he delivered it over 6,000 times during his lifetime in hundreds of American cities. It is today considered one of the
best examples of how successful Americans of the Gilded Age saw their
world. The theme was that every man should look about him for
opportunities, work hard to take advantage of those opportunities, and

grow rich. That was the "ideal" toward which every man should direct
his life. The Christian virtues of charity and compassion are conspicu-
ously missing from Conwell's philosophy.

Conwell always began his speech with a story, which he said was
told to him by an Arab guide as he made a journey down the Tigris and
Euphrates Rivers.

The old guide told me that there once lived not far from the River
Indus an ancient Persian by the name of Ali Hafed. He said that Ali
Hafed owned a very large farm, that he had orchards, grain-fields,
and gardens; that he had money at interest, and was a wealthy and
contented man. He was contented because he was wealthy, and
wealthy because he was contented. One day there visited that old
Persian farmer one of those ancient Buddhist priests, one of the
wise men of the East. He sat down by the fire and told this old
farmer of ours how the world was made. He said that this world
was once a mere bank of fog, and that the Almighty thrust His finger
into this bank of fog, and began slowly to move his finger around,
increasing the speed until at last it fell in floods of rain upon its hot
surface, and cooled the outward crust. Then the internal fires bursting outward through the crust threw up the mountains and hills, the
valleys, the plains and prairies of this wonderful world of ours. If
this internal molten mass came bursting out and cooled very quickly it became granite; less quickly copper, less quickly silver, less
quickly gold, and, after gold, diamonds were made.

Said the old priest, "A diamond is a congealed drop of sunlight."
Now that is literally scientifically true, that a diamond is an actual
deposit of carbon from the sun. The old priest told Ali Hafed that if
he had one diamond the size of his thumb he could purchase the
country, and if he had a mine of diamonds he could place his children upon thrones through the influence of their great wealth.

Ali Hafed heard all about diamonds, how much they were worth,
and went to bed that night a poor man. He had not lost anything,
but he was poor because he was discontented, and discontented
because he feared he was poor. He said, "I want a mine of diamonds," and he lay awake all night.

Early in the morning he sought out the priest. I know by experience that a priest is very cross when awakened early in the morning, and when he shook that old priest out of his dreams, Ali Hafed
said to him:

"Will you tell me where I can find diamonds?"

"Diamonds! What do you want with diamonds?" "Why, I wish to
be immensely rich." "Well, then, go along and find them. That is all
you have to do; go and find them, and then you have them." "But I
don't know where to go." "Well, if you will find a river that runs

through white sands, between high mountains, in those white sands you will always find diamonds." "I don't believe there is any such river." "Oh yes, there are plenty of them. All you have to do is to go and find them, and then you have them." Said Ali Hafed, "I will go."

So he sold his farm, collected his money, left his family in charge of a neighbor, and away he went in search of diamonds. He began his search, very properly to my mind, at the Mountains of the Moon. Afterward he came around into Palestine, then wandered on into Europe, and at last when his money was all spent and he was in rags, wretchedness, and poverty, he stood on the shore of that bay at Barcelona, in Spain, when a great tidal wave came rolling in between the pillars of Hercules, and the poor, afflicted, suffering, dying man could not resist the awful temptation to cast himself into that incoming tide, and he sank beneath its foaming crest, never to rise in this life again.

———

The man who purchased Ali Hafed's farm one day led his camel into the garden to drink, and as that camel put its nose into the shallow water of that garden brook, Ali Hafed's successor noticed a curious flash of light from the white sands of the stream. He pulled out a black stone having an eye of light reflecting all the hues of the rainbow. He took the pebble into the house and put it on the mantel which covers the central fires, and forgot all about it.

A few days later this same old priest came in to visit Ali Hafed's successor, and the moment he opened that drawing-room door he saw that flash of light on the mantel, and he rushed up to it, and shouted: "Here is a diamond! Has Ali Hafed returned?" "Oh no, Ali Hafed has not returned, and that is not a diamond. That is nothing but a stone we found right out here in our garden." "But," said the priest, "I tell you I know a diamond when I see it. I know positively that is a diamond."

Then together they rushed out into that old garden and stirred up the white sands with their fingers, and lo! There came up other more beautiful and valuable gems than the first. "Thus," said the guide to me, and, friends, it is historically true, "was discovered the diamond mine of Golconda, the most magnificent diamond-mine in all the history of mankind, excelling the Kimberly itself. The Kohinoor, and the Orloff of the crown jewels of England and Russia, the largest on earth, came from that mine."

Conwell always ended his story with this moral: had Ali Hafed stayed at home and dug in his own garden, instead of wasting his wealth and life searching abroad, he would have found acres of diamonds. Under the very land he abandoned lay enough gems to decorate the crowns of all the world's monarchs. Then Conwell gave American

examples: a man who sold his home in northern California to
Johann Sutter, who promptly found gold there, to go in search of
riches; a man who sold his land in Titusville, Pennsylvania, where
Edwin Drake soon discovered oil, in order to take a job in Canada
working at an hourly wage for an oil company; and a mining major
at Yale who sold land in Massachusetts, where one of the largest silver strikes was later made, in order to head west to search for copper. All of which demonstrated that a man should look for wealth
beneath his feet. The opportunity to get rich, Conwell said with
righteous conviction, was at hand. Then he defended the acquisitive
nature of man as a Christian virtue.

> I say that you ought to get rich, and it is your duty to get rich. How
> many of my pious brethren say to me, "Do you, a Christian minister,
> spend your time going up and down the country advising young
> people to get rich, to get money?" "Yes, of course I do." They say,
> "Isn't that awful! Why don't you preach the gospel instead of
> preaching about man's making money?" "Because to make money
> honestly is to preach the gospel." That is the reason. The men who
> get rich may be the most honest men you find in the community.
>
> "Oh," but says some young man here to-night, "I have been told
> all my life that if a person has money he is very dishonest and dis-
> honorable and mean and contemptible." My friend, that is the rea-
> son why you have none, because you have that idea of people. The
> foundation of your faith is altogether false. Let me say here clearly,
> and say it briefly, though subject to discussion which I have not
> time for here, ninety-eight out of one hundred of the rich men of
> America are honest. That is why they are rich. That is why they are
> trusted with money. That is why they carry on great enterprises
> and find plenty of people to work with them. It is because they
> are honest men.
>
> Says another young man, "I hear sometimes of men that get mil-
> lions of dollars dishonestly." Yes, of course you do, and so do I. But
> they are so rare a thing in fact that the news-papers talk about them
> all the time as a matter of news until you get the idea that all the
> other rich men got rich dishonestly.
>
> My friend, you take and drive me—if you furnish the auto—out
> into the suburbs of Philadelphia, and introduce me to the people
> who own their homes around this great city, those beautiful homes
> with gardens and flowers, those magnificent homes so lovely in
> their art, and I will introduce you to the very best people in charac-
> ter as well as in enterprise in our city, and you know I will. A man is
> not really a true man until he owns his own home, and they that
> own their homes are made more honorable and honest and pure,
> and true and economical and careful, by owning the home.

For a man to have money, even in large sums, is not an inconsistent thing. We preach against covetousness, and you know we do, in the pulpit, and oftentimes preach against it so long and use the terms about "filthy lucre" so extremely that Christians get the idea that when we stand in the pulpit we believe it is wicked for any man to have money—until the collection basket goes around, and then we almost swear at the people because they don't give more money. Oh, the inconsistency of such doctrines as that!

Money is power, and you ought to be reasonably ambitious to have it. You ought because you can do more good with it than you could without it. Money printed your Bible, money builds your churches, money sends your missionaries, and money pays your preachers, and you would not have many of them, either, if you did not pay them. I am always willing that my church should raise my salary, because the church that pays the largest salary always raises it the easiest. You never knew an exception to it in your life. The man who gets the largest salary can do the most good with the power that is furnished to him. Of course he can if his spirit is right to use it for what it is given to him.

I say, then, you ought to have money. If you can honestly attain unto riches in Philadelphia, it is your Christian and godly duty to do so. It is an awful mistake of these pious people to think you must be awfully poor in order to be pious.

Some men say, "Don't you sympathize with the poor people?" Of course I do, or else I would not have been lecturing these years. I won't give in but what I sympathize with the poor, but the number of poor who are to be sympathized with is very small. To sympathize with a man whom God has punished for his sins, thus to help him when God would still continue a just punishment, is to do wrong, no doubt about it, and we do that more than we help those who are deserving. While we should sympathize with God's poor—that is, those who cannot help themselves—let us remember there is not a poor person in the United States who was not made poor by his own shortcomings, or by the shortcomings of someone else. It is all wrong to be poor, anyhow . . .

Conwell's form of Christianity was ideally suited to the affluent America of the late nineteenth century.

BLACK ASPIRATIONS: BOOKER T. WASHINGTON'S ATLANTA EXPOSITION ADDRESS

Russell Conwell was himself a prosperous man. He lived among prosperous men, raised money for his hospital and college by appealing to prosperous men for funds, and his message pleased prosperous men. Yet his sermon and its theme appealed also to the masses of Americans, many of them poor, who wanted to believe that they too could find diamonds. It even found resonance among leaders in the African-American community, the most economically disadvantaged of American citizens. It was heard in the speeches of Booker T. Washington, the founder of Tuskegee Institute, a training school for poor southern blacks in Alabama. Washington encouraged his people to seek economic prosperity before demanding civil equality, and he believed such material prosperity was possible. Washington admired the spirit and achievements of Andrew Carnegie and those like him, and he encouraged his people to imitate them.

Washington delivered the following speech on September 18, 1895, at the "colored" pavilion of the Cotton and International Exposition in Atlanta, Georgia. It has been called a "compromise" with the white power structure of the South, which after the emancipation of the slaves adopted a policy of strict segregation by race. In it Washington assured his white audience, who sat in front seats while blacks sat in the back—at their own pavilion—that agitating for immediate social equality was folly and that artificially enforcing integration of the races would not work. It was important for black people to have legal privileges, he said, but they must prepare themselves for equality first by achieving the American dream of affluence. "The opportunity to earn a dollar in a factory just now is worth infinitely more than the opportunity to spend a dollar in an opera house," he said that day. These words both encouraged blacks and reassured whites. Begin at the bottom, Washington said, and work your way up. You can.

Just as significantly, and often overlooked both by his white audience and by later black leaders who rejected his "compromise," Washington's speech reflected the philosophy expressed by Conwell in the "Acres of Diamonds" address. It was possible to get rich. America had untold wealth, and black people could and should gain as much of it as possible. That was the American ideal. Those who achieved the ideal were heroes.

A ship lost at sea for many days suddenly sighted a friendly vessel. From the mast of the unfortunate vessel was seen a signal: "Water, water; we die of thirst!" The answer from the friendly vessel at once came back: "Cast down your bucket where you are." A second time the signal, "Water, water; send us water!" ran up from the distressed vessel, and was answered: "Cast down your bucket where you are." And a third and fourth signal for water was answered, "Cast down your bucket where you are." The captain of the distressed vessel, at last heeding the injunction, cast down his bucket, and it came up full of fresh, sparkling water from the mouth of the

Amazon River. To those of my race who depend upon bettering their condition in a foreign land, or who underestimate the importance of cultivating friendly relations with the Southern white man who is their next-door neighbor, I would say: "Cast down your bucket where you are"—cast it down in making friends, in every manly way, of the people of all races by whom we are surrounded.

Cast it down in agriculture, mechanics, in commerce, in domestic service, and in the professions. And in this connection it is well to bear in mind that whatever other sins the South may be called to bear, when it comes to business, pure and simple, it is in the South that the Negro is given a man's chance in the commercial world, and in nothing is this Exposition more eloquent than in emphasizing this chance. Our greatest danger is that in the leap from slavery to freedom we may overlook the fact that the masses of us are to live by the productions of our hands, and fail to keep in mind that we shall prosper in proportion as we learn to dignify and glorify common labor, and put brains and skill into the common occupations of life; shall prosper in proportion as we learn to draw the line between the superficial and the substantial, the ornamental geegaws of life and the useful. No race can prosper till it learns that there is as much dignity in tilling a field as in writing a poem. It is at the bottom of life we must begin, and not at the top. Nor should we permit our grievances to overshadow our opportunities.

To those of the white race who look to the incoming of those of foreign birth and strange tongue and habits for the prosperity of the South, were I permitted, I would repeat what I say to my own race, "Cast down your bucket where you are." Cast it down among the eight million Negroes whose habits you know, whose fidelity and love you have tested in days when to have proved treacherous meant the ruin of your firesides. Cast down your bucket among these people who have without strikes and labor wars tilled your fields, cleared your forests, builded your railroads and cities, brought forth treasures from the bowels of the earth, and helped make possible this magnificent representation of the progress of the South. Cast down your bucket, my people, helping and encouraging them as you are doing on these grounds, and, with education of head, hand, and heart, you will find that they will buy your surplus land, make blossom the waste places in your fields, and run your factories. While doing this, you can be sure in the future, as in the past, that you and your families will be surrounded by the most patient, faithful, law abiding, and unresentful people that the world has seen. As we have proved our loyalty to you in the past, in nursing your children, watching by the sick bed of your mothers and fathers, and often following them with tear-dimmed eyes to their graves, so in the future, in our humble way, we shall stand by you with a devotion that no foreigner can approach, ready to lay down our lives, if need be, in defense of yours, interlacing our industrial, commercial, civil, and religious life with yours in a way that shall make the interests of both races one. In all things that are purely social we can be as separate as the fingers, yet one as the hand in all things essential to mutual progress.

Washington called on his people to cast down their buckets just as Conwell called on his to search for diamonds. They both spoke for the American dream of riches.

A WARNING FROM MARK TWAIN: STORIES OF GOOD AND BAD LITTLE BOYS

Even the Americans with the least hope of becoming fabulously rich were thus urged to believe in the American dream of riches, to reach for their piece of the pie, even if that piece seemed small and elusive. This was the dominant American philosophy of the day.

While the philosophy was dominant, it was not unquestioned. Alger, Conwell, and Washington did not represent the thinking of all Americans. There were some people, white and black, native born and immigrant, who questioned the rosy scenario of the "poor boy who strikes it rich." African-American writer W. E. B. DuBois warned about the racism that stood in the way of black people's success. White writers warned that the dream of riches did not find fulfillment in the lives of many people; that those who did get rich often did so not because of their honesty but indeed because of their dishonesty; and that once they were rich and powerful they often showed little concern for the people they left behind and whose labor made them rich. The popular author Mark Twain raised many questions about the American dream of riches as he challenged the Horatio Alger myth.

In "The Story of the Bad Little Boy," which Twain wrote in 1865, the little boy Jim was not raised in poverty, and his mother neither died and left him an orphan nor took him to Sunday School. He stole jam from the pantry and apples from the trees and never got caught. He stole his teacher's penknife and deftly blamed the theft on another boy. He constantly broke the Sabbath peace and never suffered punishment. Finally, "he grew up and married, and raised a large family, and brained them all with an ax one night, and got wealthy by all manner of cheating and rascality; and now he is the infernalest, wickedest scoundrel in his native village, and is universally respected, and belongs to the legislature." So much for the idea that poor, honest, moral boys were the ones who made good.

In "The Story of the Good Little Boy," written in 1870, Twain challenged the other side of the myth. The little boy Jacob obeyed his parents, lived an exemplary moral life, and longed to be the subject of a Sunday School book story. But his efforts all proved futile. A blind man he tried to help, instead of blessing him, blamed him for his woes. A dog he tried to befriend tore his clothes off. Attempting to warn a bad boy against taking a cruise on the Sabbath, he fell into the water and spent nine weeks in bed sick. Finally, in trying to release fifteen dogs some bad little boys were about to tie to cans of nitroglycerin, he was blown into a thousand pieces and scattered across the county. "Thus perished the good little boy who did the best he could, but didn't come out according to the books. Every boy who ever did as he did prospered except him. His case is truly remarkable. It will probably never be accounted for."

Tongue planted firmly in cheek, Twain was challenging the most popular myth of his day. His prestige gave his stories credibility and raised doubts in intellectual circles. He came closest to a direct spoof of the Horatio Alger–Andrew Carnegie story when he wrote "Life As I Found It" in 1874, which was published under the title "Poor Little Stephen Girard" in the magazine *Carleton's Popular Readings* in 1879. Still a popular work, it has recently been reissued as an illustrated book for young readers. Stephen Girard was neither a good nor a bad boy, just naive, just a believer in the American dream.

> The man lived in Philadelphia who, when young and poor, entered a bank, and says he: "Please, sir, don't you want a boy?" And the stately personage said "No, little boy, I don't want a little boy." The little boy, whose heart was too full for utterance, chewing a piece of licorice stick he had bought with a cent stolen from his good and pious aunt, with sobs plainly audible, and with great globules of water rolling down his cheeks, glided silently down the marble steps of the bank. Bending his noble form, the bank man dodged behind a door, for he thought the little boy was going to shy a stone at him. But the little boy picked up something, and stuck it in his poor but ragged jacket. "Come here, little boy," and the little boy did come here; and the bank man said: "Lo, what pickest thou up?" and he answered and replied: "A pin." and the bank man said: "Little boy, are you good?" and he said he was. And the bank man said: "How do you vote?—excuse me, do you go to Sunday school?" and he said he did. Then the bank man took down a pen made of pure gold, and flowing with pure ink, and he wrote on a piece of paper, "St. Peter"; and he asked the little boy what it stood for, and he said "Salt Peter." Then the bankman said it meant "Saint Peter." The little boy said: "Oh!"

Then the bank man took the little boy to his bosom, and the little boy said "Oh!" again, for he squeezed him. Then the bank man took the little boy into partnership, and gave him half the profits and all the capital, and he married the bank man's daughter, and now all he has is all his, and all his own too.

My uncle told me this story, and I spent six weeks in picking up pins in front of a bank. I expected the bank man would call me in and say: "Little boy, are you good?" and I was going to say "Yes"; and when he asked me what "St. John" stood for, I was going to say "Salt John." But the bank man wasn't anxious to have a partner, and I guess the daughter was a son, for one day says he to me: "Little boy, what's that you're picking up?" Says I, awfully meekly, "Pins." Says he: "Let's see 'em," and he took 'em, and I took off my cap, all ready to go in the bank, and become a partner, and marry his daughter. But I didn't get an invitation. He said: "Those pins belong to the bank, and if I catch you hanging around here any more I'll set the dog on you!" Then I left, and the mean old fellow kept the pins. Such is life as I find it.

Twain probably took gleeful delight in naming his naïve little boy Stephen Girard after the French-born Philadelphia multimillionaire. The real Stephen Girard was to many people an epiphany of the American success story, but Twain knew better. In 1874 the name Andrew Carnegie was not among the list of fabulously wealthy American entrepreneurs; but the cautionary elements in Twain's story apply to all the high achievers of the entire Gilded Age. Twain never did in fact openly ridicule Carnegie and his success story, in part perhaps because and he and Carnegie were in agreement about one major issue of the last years of the nineteenth century. They were both opposed to the "imperialism" that threatened to create an American Empire. But his stories questioned the Carnegie mythology.

HISTORIAN HAROLD LIVESAY LOOKS AT CARNEGIE'S RISE

Since he was one of the best examples of the nineteenth-century vision of the American dream, in many ways the American ideal of his day, historians have found Carnegie an intriguing person to study. The best of their biographies are balanced and objective. They neither condemn nor praise him. Most of them agree with Carnegie himself that the key to his success lay in the challenges of his early years and the way he reacted to them, both in Scotland and in Pittsburgh, as he took his first steps from poverty to wealth. For example, the historian Louis Hacker wrote in *The World of Andrew Carnegie*:

> Because of his father's failure, because of his deep devotion to a mother who kept the little family together in its early years of struggle, perhaps more because of the unequal society from which he had come and which had squandered talent so stupidly, Carnegie had a fierce desire to succeed. He had to sharpen his wits; he had to engage in self-improvement; he had to seize the main chance whenever it presented itself. How else was one like himself to emerge out of obscurity and poverty? (p. 60)

Yet historians also caution that such things do not fully explain his stupendous success or the drive to continue his accumulation of money far beyond his own personal needs. Early poverty does not explain his "gift" for acquisition or his great pleasure, often leading to embarrassment and guilt, in becoming not just rich but fabulously rich.

One of the most able historians to examine Carnegie's early years was Harold Livesay. In his book *Andrew Carnegie and the Rise of Big Business,* first published in 1975 and reissued in 2000, he examined the life of the wee Scots boy who made it so big in his adopted America.

> Joining the railroad at the age of seventeen, Carnegie had thus already exhibited most of the qualities that would carry him to wealth and power. In addition to working so hard and believing in his own destiny, he had enough charisma to persuade others to follow him. He made the right friends; he admired strength and despised weakness. Although loyal, kind, and independent in his dealings with most people, he showed streaks of guile and obsequiousness now and again. Physically durable (an asset often underrated as a component of success) and mentally acute; he had a retentive memory and an uncanny instinct for opportunity. The years in the telegraph office put these qualities through a basic training in business, adding acquired techniques to inherent talent. The railroad presented an unprecedented challenge; he assaulted it with the same restless ambition he had always shown.
>
> And what made Andy run? Why did he feel that "whatever I engage in I must push inordinately"? Certain obvious factors suggest themselves. He was a small boy and a short man (five-feet-three-inches full-grown at a time when the average American male stood five-feet-seven). His father was a weak parent and his mother a strong one. Andrew felt driven to prove his manhood and he had to compete with his brother for his mother's love. Success in the business world soothed his self-doubts and the guilt feelings that afflicted many immigrants.

Emigration usually was an admission of an inability to cope with life at home. No matter how severe the vicissitudes that prompted their departure, expatriates often felt that their own shortcomings had played a major part. As a result, many immigrants felt driven to prove themselves in their new country, to show the folks at home that having failed once they could succeed on the second try. Margaret and Andrew Carnegie both dreamed of the day when they could re-turn in triumph to Dunfermline. The most splendid occa-sion—perhaps the most satisfying moment of Margaret Carnegie's life—came in 1881 when Carnegie presented his birthplace with a new library. The city held a commemorative parade, eight thousand marchers strong, with banners reading "Welcome Carnegie, Generous Son." Mother and son brought up the rear of the procession, riding in a palatial coach-and-four, passing in triumph through the town they had once fled in poverty.

During his first few years in the United States, Carnegie's letters home bristled with vindication of the family's move. Each advance in salary and every promotion provided an occasion for a sermon (usu-ally directed to Cousin Dod Lauder) on the virtues of the new coun-try. "We have all of your good traits," Carnegie wrote, "and few of your bad ones . . . We go ahead. I would have been a poor weaver all my days, but here, I can surely do something better . . . if I don't it will be my own fault, for anyone can get along in this country." At Uncle Lauder's prompting, he and his cousin carried on an epistolary debate on the relative merits of the two countries' political systems. Carnegie leaped nimbly over such faults as slavery and dwelt at length on what he saw as the republic's merits: its free press, small military and police forces, cheap postal service, upright politicians, freedom from stultifying traditions, willingness to innovate.

But greatest of all its virtues was the democratic political process and the economic benefits derived from it: "We now possess what the working classes of Your Country look forward to as constituting their political millennium. We have the charter which you have been fighting for for years as the panacea for all Britain's woes, the bulwark of the liberties of the people." Possession of the charter, Carnegie thought, made America's economic dominance inevitable: "The best proof of the superiority of our system is seen in the gen-eral prosperity." The national treasury held a surplus; the public debt was paid as it matured; the western lands were filling up; 13,000 miles of railroad and 21,000 miles of telegraph had been built with thousands more on the way; pauperism rarely occurred. These bene-fits derived from the government that existed by the consent of the governed . . .

All his life Carnegie adhered to this theme of the interdepend-ence between political equality and economic superiority. This equation served Carnegie as a two-edged sword: with one side he attacked other countries' systems as inferior; with the other he defended American institutions against criticism. In the United States most things were right; those which were not would improve or disappear because the system was self-correcting. This handy credo excused all kinds of economic abuses and justified opposition to economic reforms either by government intervention or by labor agitation. If the business world reformed, then, Carnegie argued, it would inevitably come as a consequence of the political system. Carnegie clung to this belief despite demonstrations of extensive political corruption and evidence of widespread economic abuse, including some perpetrated by Carnegie himself.

Joseph Wall, Carnegie's most exhaustive biographer, explains Carnegie's attitudes more as a result of "arrested development" than of hypocrisy. Carnegie left Scotland before systematic doctrines of economic reform such as socialism came into public consciousness. He espoused Scottish Radicalism, largely expressed in opposition to the Corn Laws (a tariff on imported grain), support of the Charter, and "death to privilege" (abolition of hereditary aristocracies).

Americans had long since attained these goals, and Carnegie "looked no further into the meaning of liberalism." Undoubtedly this accounted for Carnegie's rationale. His obstinate adherence to it in the face of massive contradictions—he was, after all, neither unobservant, stupid, unfeeling, nor incapable of changing— bespoke a deeper emotion, rooted in a personal commitment. Also, he defended the American system so vigorously because its triumph was his own triumph; its virtues were his virtues; and its success justified his wealth and the ways he acquired it. Attacks on the system attacked him. If the system were virtuous, then Carnegie was a Horatio Alger hero personified; if the system were evil, then he had traded his Scottish birthright for a mess of American pottage and left his fellow Scots to fight for the Charter while he himself focused on making himself rich.

But even after all these things are said, the ultimate source of Carnegie's consuming ambition remains elusive. Plenty of undersized Scottish immigrant boys had parents who reversed roles, sibling jealousies, and self-doubts without evincing Andrew Carnegie's relentless yearning for power. . . .

BILL GATES ON THE RAGS TO RICHES MYTH IN CONTEMPORARY AMERICA

Whatever his motivations, opportunities, and personal skills at accumulating wealth, Carnegie's rags to riches story—as the perfect example of what was even before his day the American dream—caught and held the imagination of the American public, making him an unforgettable American ideal. Long after he retired, after he became a philanthropist, after the federal government moved to curb monopolies such as he had established, the story of the poor Scottish boy who became the richest man in the world was told to young people to show them what they could do in life. As late as 1966 a book by Joanne Landers Henry titled *Andrew Carnegie, Young Steelmaker* held him up as a heroic figure for American youth. In her book the young Andrew was a true Horatio Alger figure. Trying to sell gooseberries on a Dunfermline street, he stopped a runaway horse and saved a child's life but refused a reward. All he asked of his admirers was that they buy his berries. He was already brave, honest, and a master salesman. He was on his way to fame and fortune. The book contained a drawing of the adult Carnegie walking through one of his steel mills, accepting the grateful smiles of his laborers, already dreaming of the day when he would retire and spend his time giving his fortune away to provide these men with public libraries.

For the first half of the twentieth century, due to the passage of a graduated income tax and governmental regulations of industry, it was said that there would be no more Carnegies, no more men who would start from scratch and become multimillionaires. The Great Depression, with its bankruptcies and neo-poverty, seemd to confirm this assumption. But the post–World War II building boom, fueled by the Cold War, the baby boom, and the computer revolution, proved that assumption false. Perhaps the best example of a man of relatively modest means who in this new age became fabulously rich is Bill Gates. Gates was not born poor. In fact he attended a private high school and then Harvard University, which he left before graduating to begin manufacturing computers. Luck played a part in Gates' story, as did his vision to take advantage of an opportunity, but he is a modern success story. If we compare his present fortune to that of the family in which he grew up, he has indeed come from rags to riches. Gates, aware of the poor boy who strikes it rich myth, likes to describe his journey as one that began on a "shoestring" and led to wealth.

In his book *The Road Ahead* he recounted how as a boy he came to be fascinated by the primitive computer machines that made their appearance during his school days, and how as a university student he started the company called Microsoft. By the late 1990s Microsoft had made him one of the world's richest men and the object of governmental probes of what critics called Microsoft's monopolistic practices.

> I wrote my first software program when I was thirteen years old. It was for playing tic-tac-toe. The computer I was using was huge and cumbersome and slow and absolutely compelling.

Letting a bunch of teenagers loose on a computer was the idea of the Mothers' Club at Lakeside, the private school I attended. The mothers decided that the proceeds from a rummage sale should be used to install a terminal and buy computer time for students. Letting students use a computer in the late 1960's was a pretty amazing choice at the time in Seattle—and one I'll always be grateful for.

This computer terminal didn't have a screen. To play, we typed in our moves on a type-writer-style keyboard and then sat around until the results came chug-chugging out of a loud printing device on paper. Then we'd rush over to take a look and see who'd won or decide our next move. A game of tic-tac-toe, which would take thirty seconds with a pencil and paper, might consume most of a lunch period. But who cared? There was something neat about the machine.

I realized later part of the appeal was that here was an enormous, expensive, grown-up machine and we, the kids, could control it. We were too young to drive or to do any of the other fun-seeming adult activities, but we could give this big machine orders and it would always obey. Computers are great because when you're working with them you get immediate results that let you know if your program works. It's feedback you don't get from many other things. That was the beginning of my fascination with software. The feedback from simple programs is particularly unambiguous. And to this day it still thrills me to know that if I can get the program right it will always work perfectly, every time, just the way I told it to.

———

Of course, in those days we were just goofing around, or so we thought. But the toy we had—well, it turned out to be some toy. A few of us at Lakeside refused to quit playing with it. In the minds of a lot of people at school we became linked with the computer, and it with us. I was asked by a teacher to help teach computer programming, and that seemed to be OK with everyone. But when I got the lead in the school play, *Black Comedy,* some students were muttering, "Why did they pick the computer guy?" That's still the way I sometimes get identified.

It seems there was a whole generation of us, all over the world, who dragged that favorite toy with us into adulthood. In doing so, we caused a kind of revolution—peaceful, mainly—and now the computer has taken up residence in our offices and homes. . . .

In 1975, when he was a student at Harvard, he and his friend Paul Allen, also a computer nerd, decided to start a company of their own. Gates said that they were like two kids in one of the old Judy Garland–Mickey Rooney films, plotting how they could put on a show in the garage. In five weeks of intensive work they produced an operating system that they marketed under the company name of Microsoft.

We knew getting a company started would mean sacrifice. But we also realized we had to do it then or forever lose the opportunity to make it in microcomputer software. In the spring of 1975, Paul quit his programming job and I decided to go on leave from Harvard.

I talked it over with my parents, both of whom were pretty savvy about business. They saw how much I wanted to try starting a software company and they were supportive. My plan was to take time off, start the company, and then go back later and finish college. I never really made a conscious decision to forgo a degree. Technically, I'm just on a really long leave. Unlike some students, I loved college. I thought it was fun to sit around and talk with so many smart people my own age. However, I felt the window of opportunity to start a software company might not open again. So I dove into the world of business when I was nineteen years old.

From the start, Paul and I funded everything ourselves. Each of us had saved some money. Paul had been well paid at Honeywell, and some of the money I had came from late-night poker games in the dorm. Fortunately, our company didn't require massive funding.

People often ask me to explain Microsoft's success. They want to know the secret of getting from a two-man, shoestring operation to a company with 17,000 employees and more than $6 billion a year in sales. Of course, there is no simple answer, and luck played a role, but I think the most important element was our original vision.

We glimpsed what lay beyond that Intel 8080 chip, and then acted on it. We asked, "What if computing were nearly free?" We believed there would be computers everywhere because of cheap computing power and great new software that would take advantage of it. We set up shop betting on the former and producing the latter when no one else was. Our initial insight made everything else a bit easier. We were in the right place at the right time. We got there first and our early success gave us the chance to hire many smart people. We built a worldwide sales force and used the revenue it generated to fund new products. From the beginning we set off down a road that was headed in the right direction.

A *Newsweek* magazine poll taken in the year 2000 found that for the emerging Generation Y—the children of Generation X and grandchildren of the Baby Boomers—Bill Gates is the most admired living American. He was named first in the poll, among eleven public figures, by an overwhelming 48% of those surveyed. At the beginning of the twenty-first century, the story of the poor boy who strikes it rich is still the American ideal, just as he was at the beginning of the twentieth century. Then it was Andrew Carnegie; now it is Bill Gates.

QUESTIONS FOR CRITICAL EXAMINATION

1. What do Carnegie's articles and speeches on his early life and career reveal about him as a person and businessman? How did he account for his success? What part did factors such as personal motivation, opportunity, and luck play in his success? What accounts for his "knack" of accumulating wealth? Why he and not others?

2. Explain Carnegie's attitude about the value of early poverty? What logical sense does it make? What contradictions do you find in his argument? How do you feel his speech about starting at the bottom (e.g., sweeping floors) would play to an audience of college students today?

3. How is the Horatio Alger story you read similar to the story of Andrew Carnegie, and how is it different? What characteristics did Alger say would lead a poor boy to fame and fortune? Which of those did Carnegie have, and which did he not have? What kind of myths about the American dream did Alger create and perpetuate? How much were his characters like people you know?

4. How does Conwell's "Acres of Diamonds" address reflect the prevailing philosophy of his day? How did he justify encouraging Christians to accumulate wealth? How might a minister from a congregation in a poor part of Philadelphia have taken Conwell to task about his theory that wealth came to the godly?

5. Explain how Mark Twain used biting satire to attack the rags to riches myth. What made Twain want to call the myth into question? How do you think his readers reacted to his attack on the American dream?

6. Using Harold Livesay's interpretation of Carnegie's early life, show how a historian takes historical data and draws logical conclusions from them. In what ways does Livesay go beyond the facts and impose his own assumptions on Carnegie's story? Does he go too far, or would you have liked him to go farther and give more such interpretation?

7. In what ways do Bill Gates and his story remind you of Andrew Carnegie and his story, and in what ways are they different? What parts did intelligence, opportunity, and luck play in Gates success? How are entrepreneurs like Carnegie and Gates both complex and simplistic in their attitude toward opportunity and the achievement of wealth?

Chapter Three

___

THE TYCOON: ANDREW CARNEGIE AS AMERICAN ICON

"Put all your eggs in one basket—and watch that basket!"

ANDREW CARNEGIE
New York Tribune, 1890

In 1872, already a wealthy man at the age of 35, Andrew Carnegie observed firsthand the potential productivity and financial gain of a new method of turning iron into steel, a method perfected by the man he always called the "crazy Frenchman," Henry Bessemer. The Bessemer Method revolutionized American industry and made Carnegie fabulously rich. With an investment of $700,000 ($250,000 of it with his own money) he opened the first American steel mill. The next year brought a financial panic which affected all American industry, but Carnegie sold his stock in other concerns to protect his new investment, which survived and quickly began to flourish. Because it was both lighter and stronger than iron, steel was indeed the product of the future, and Carnegie was out in front of other steel producers. In 1886 he consolidated several steel and coke firms (coke was the material that created heat intense enough to purify iron into steel) and quickly rose to the top of the industrial ladder. That year Carnegie Brothers and Company made $2,925,350 in profits. In 1892 it made $4,000,000, and its holdings were valued at $25,000,000. In 1898 the profits were over $10,000,000. In 1900, when Carnegie retired and sold his company's holdings to a consortium that became United States Steel, the holdings were worth nearly $400,000,000. Three-quarters of the profits from his steel works went into his own pockets. At the turn of the twentieth century Andrew Carnegie was the world's richest man.

His move from Scotland to America was extraordinarily fortuitous. In the United States men like Carnegie had far more freedom to gain great wealth than they had in Europe. America was rich in natural resources; the U.S. government favored business leaders; and labor unions were weak and ineffective. In Europe at the same time there were stronger laws to protect workers and prevent exploitation of men and resources. The work and eventual effectiveness of such groups as the Chartists, which Carnegie's family supported, assured that Carnegie could not have made so great a fortune in Britain as he did in America.

As Carnegie was growing rich and powerful, the Darwinian theory of evolution was being debated across Europe and America. Darwin argued that plant and animal species of modern times survived across the eons and rose to dominance because they were fittest to live in the natural environment. Darwin inspired Herbert Spencer to postulate that modern human society was also the product of long evolution in which the fittest humans rose to dominance in governance, scholarship, and economics. Carnegie eagerly lapped up this theory, met with Spencer to discuss it, and came to see himself as a prime example of "Social Darwinism." As the years passed and Carnegie rose to be the world's richest man, more and more Americans came to agree with him.

The "will to power" is a universal human characteristic. People seek power to satisfy their physical needs, to control others, to do good or ill, or a combination of the three. Power through the ages has been achieved by wielding brute force, by exercising moral or religious persuasion, and/or by controlling the distribution and productivity of land. In the nineteenth century, however, as Carnegie's career unfolded, power came more and more to lie in the ability to control transferable products; and the most powerful men were the tycoons who transferred them. No one was more adept at capturing and wielding such power than the Scots immigrant who became the "emperor of steel." He was the nineteenth-century tycoon *par excellence.*

CARNEGIE AS THE EMPEROR OF STEEL

By 1872 Carnegie had put all his eggs in the steel basket, and from that basket he drew his immense wealth. He never learned the technical details of steel manufacturing. He seldom visited one of his mills, offering the excuse that he was unable to stand the heat they produced. He raised the money to run his company, oversaw modernizations of his plants that made them ever more productive, and kept a sharp eye on markets to make certain his profits would continue to pour in. Manufacturing itself did not interest him, and neither really did management. His passion was the accumulation of wealth. Yet from the beginning of his career he was of two minds. He reveled in making money, yet he seemed always to have felt some guilt about making so much of it, particularly at the expense of laboring men with whom he claimed kinship. At the same time, while he was making his fortune, he longed to live a life of the mind by reading and writing books, and carrying on conversations and correspondences with intellectuals.

From childhood he had borrowed books to read; and when he was able to buy them, he began to accumulate his own collection. It was said that he could recite by heart all the works of the Scottish poet Robert Burns and long passages from Shakespeare. He sought out such men as Herbert Spencer and Mark Twain and shared his thoughts with them. Through monetary gifts he earned invitations to speak and receive honorary degrees from the finest universities in America and Britain. He wrote and published books which displayed an impressive degree of literary and philosophical talent, along with shameless displays of self-promotion.

He also understood the benefits of leisure for intellectual development. He made his first return visit to Scotland, "on holiday" he called it, while still a railroad employee during the Civil War; and throughout his career he left business concerns behind to travel, most of the time back to Britain, once to circle the world to study diverse cultures. To the end of his life he valued his times of reflection, and the books and articles that resulted from them prove how productive they were for him.

Although his younger brother Thomas married and sired a family, Andrew remained a bachelor for half a century, living with and caring for his widowed mother. There was a tacit understanding between them that he would not marry as long as she lived. He dedicated his first widely reviewed book *Triumphant Democracy* to ". . . my favorite Heroine My Mother." He cared deeply for Louise Whitfield, the daughter of a financial colleague, but only when his mother died in 1886, the same year he lost his brother Thomas, did he propose marriage to her. When they married in 1887 he was 51, she was 30. Ten years later, when he was 61 and Louise was 40, they had their only child, a daughter who was named Margaret for his mother. He confided to intimates that he carefully avoided further pregnancies because of the risks in those days to women in childbirth.

In addition to a New York City mansion at 2 East 91st Street, he purchased and modernized Skibo Castle in northeastern Scotland, where he

Brown Brothers, Sterling. PA.

Carnegie in his tweeds at Skibo Castle, 1914.

spent as many summers as possible, living the life of a Scottish "laird," despite having so often condemned aristocracy. Located on the Firth of Dornock, eight miles from the nearest rail station at Bonar Bridge, it provided him and his small family with the isolation he craved from business and industrial concerns. He started what would be his philanthropic enterprise by making donations to his hometown of Dunfermline to build a library and a park, gratuitously riding next to his mother in a parade honoring him as the city's most successful son. After purchasing Skibo he gave many more gifts to Scottish causes. Only in 1916, when the threat of submarine attacks and his own advancing age prevented him from making further transatlantic voyages, did he end his visits to Skibo. That year he bought a country home in Lenox, Massachusetts, and called it Shadowbrook. There he died in 1919.

Thus ended the life of the man who for the last quarter of the nine-teenth century accumulated the greatest private fortune on earth. He was by far the most single-minded yet complicated of the financiers and manufacturers who called themselves captains of industry but whom their detractors called robber barons. To detractors, Carnegie was an exploiter; but to admirers he was an icon of the American dream.

CARNEGIE'S ACCOUNT OF BUILDING AND RUNNING HIS EMPIRE

Since he was the most reflective and articulate of the industrial giants, because he wrote so many articles and books and gave so many speeches, most of them about his own business career, it is clear what Carnegie thought and what he wanted the public to think about the acquisition and management of his empire. The following excerpts are revealing, both in what they said and did not say, both in the advice they gave to readers and the interpretations they imposed on histori-cal fact. He loved playing the role of sage commentator on the glori-ous field of industry.

Carnegie always spoke positively about the world of business and his place in it. No private doubts or reservations escaped his well-for-tified mind. For example, in an address to students at Cornell University [a beneficiary of his largesse] on January 11, 1896 (recounted in his book *The Empire of Business*), he said: "I can confidently recommend to you the business career as one in which there is abundant room for the exercise of man's highest power, and of every good quality in human nature. I believe the career of the great merchant, or banker, or captain of industry, to be favourable to the development of the powers of the mind, and to the ripening of the judgment upon a wide range of general subjects; to freedom from prejudice, and to the keeping of an open mind . . . ." In conclusion he said, "The business man, pure and simple plunges into and tosses upon the waves of human affairs with-out a life-preserver in the shape of a salary; he risks all. . . . The business man pursues fortune." Carnegie saw the businessman—himself the prototype—as a romantic figure, an "Indiana Jones" of industry.

Carnegie may have considered his work romantic and conducive to intellectual development, but he did not always find it smooth sail-ing. He spent a great deal of time trying to iron out the rough spots, to justify his work to himself and the general public. The following speech is one Carnegie gave to the men who worked for him at his

Homestead, Pennsylvania, steel mill, the scene of a strike in 1892 that ended in bloodshed. The speech was given at the dedication of a library and social club he built for the men at the plant, his way of assuaging some of his guilt over the incident (see Chapter 4 for details about what happened at Homestead). Eight years later he was still convinced of the speech's merits and offered it for publication to the *New York Journal*. In it he advanced a philosophy of ideal industrial cooperation, using the image of a three-legged stool, putting business in the most attractive light. There were, however, implicit admissions of imperfection in his paradise. He felt the need, for example, to warn his workers against future collective bargaining action.

> There is a partnership of three in the industrial world when an enterprise is planned. The first of these, not in importance but in time, is Capital. Without it nothing costly can be built. From it comes the first breath of life into matter, previously inert.
>
> The structures reared, equipped and ready to begin in any line of industrial activity, the second partner comes into operation. That is Business Ability. Capital has done its part. It has provided all the instrumentalities of production; but unless it can command the services of able men to manage the business, all that Capital has done crumbles into ruin.
>
> Then comes the third partner, last in order of time but not least, Labour. If it fails to perform its part, nothing can be accomplished. Capital and Business Ability, without it brought into play, are dead. The wheels cannot revolve unless the hand of Labour starts them.
>
> Now, volumes can be written as to which one of the three partners is first, second, or third in importance, and the subject will remain just as it was before. Political economists, speculative philosophers and preachers have been giving their views on the subject for hundreds of years, but the answer has not yet been found, nor can it ever be, because each of the three is all-important, and every one is equally essential to the other two. There is no first, second or last. There is no precedence! They are equal members of the great triple alliance which moves the industrial world. As a matter of history Labour existed before Capital or Business Ability, for when "Adam digged and Eve span" Adam had no capital and if one may judge from the sequel neither of the two was inordinately blessed with business ability, but this was before the reign of Industrialism began and huge investments of Capital were necessary.
>
> In our day, Capital, Business Ability, Manual Labour are the legs of a three-legged stool. While the three legs stand sound and firm, the stool stands; but let any one of the three weaken and break, let it be pulled out or struck out, down goes the stool to the ground. And the stool is of no use until the third leg is restored.

Now, the capitalist is wrong who thinks that Capital is more important than either of the other two legs. Their support is essential to him. Without them, or with only one of them, he topples over.

Business Ability is wrong when it thinks that the leg which it represents is the most important. Without the legs of Capital and Labour it is useless.

And last, let it not be forgotten that Labour also is wrong, wildly wrong, when it assumes that it is of more importance than either of the other two legs. That idea has been in the past the source of many sad mistakes.

The three are equal partners of a grand whole. Combined they work wonders; separate, neither is of much account. Thus far, notwithstanding the differences that from time to time have unfortunately rent them apart, they have made the closing century the most beneficent of all that have preceded it. Humanity, the world over, is better than it has ever been, materially and morally, and I have the faith that it is destined to reach still higher and loftier planes than even the most sanguine have imagined.

Capital, Business Ability, and Labour must be united. He is an enemy to all three who seeks to sow seeds of disunion among them.

Carnegie also believed that success in business, his own success certainly, depended upon making a worthy, dependable product. A businessman's wares must verify the maker's good name. In his *Autobiography,* published posthumously in 1924, he pointed to his first industrial venture as an example of his dedication to this principle.

The Keystone Bridge Works have always been a source of satisfaction to me. Almost every concern that had undertaken to erect iron bridges in America had failed. Many of the structures themselves had fallen and some of the worst railway disasters in America had been caused in that way. Some of the bridges had given way under wind pressure but nothing has ever happened to a Keystone bridge, and some of them have stood where the wind was not tempered. There has been no luck about it. We used only the best material and enough of it, making our own iron and later our own steel. We were our own severest inspectors, and would build a safe structure or none at all. When asked to build a bridge which we knew to be of insufficient strength or of unscientific design, we resolutely declined. Any piece of work bearing the stamp of the Keystone Bridge Works (and there are few States in the Union where such are not to be found) we were prepared to underwrite. We were as proud of our bridges as Carlyle was of the bridge his father built across the Annan. "An honest brig," as the great son rightly said.

This policy is the true secret of success. Uphill work it will be for a few years until your work is proven, but after that it is smooth sailing. Instead of objecting to inspectors they should be welcomed by all manufacturing establishments. A high standard of excellence is easily maintained, and men are educated in the effort to reach excellence. I have never known a concern to make a decided success that did not do good, honest work, and even in these days of the fiercest competition, when everything would seem to be matter of price, there lies still at the root of great business success the very much more important factor of quality. The effect of attention to quality, upon every man in the service, from the president of the concern down to the humblest laborer, cannot be overestimated. And bearing on the same question, clean, fine workshops and tools, well-kept yards and surroundings are of much greater importance than is usually supposed.

I was very much pleased to hear a remark, made by one of the prominent bankers who visited the Edgar Thomson Works [Carnegie's first mill] during a Bankers Convention held at Pittsburgh. He was one of a party of some hundreds of delegates, and after they had passed through the works he said to our manager:

"Somebody appears to belong to these works."

He put his finger there upon one of the secrets of success. They did belong to somebody. The president of an important manufacturing work once boasted to me that their men had chased away the first inspector who had ventured to appear among them, and that they had never been troubled with another since. This was said as a matter of sincere congratulation, but I thought to myself: "This concern will never stand the strain of competition; it is bound to fail when hard times come." The result proved the correctness of my belief. The surest foundation of a manufacturing concern is quality. After that, and a long way after, comes cost.

Carnegie also believed that the successful industrialist knew when to seize the moment and take advantage of an opportunity for higher profits, even when that meant compromise and merger. It was also in his *Autobiography* that he recalled the potentially unprofitable competition between his Woodruff Palace Sleeping Car Company and the newer Pullman Company. Carnegie knew that the demand for sleeping cars was great enough that the two companies would profit more by cooperation than by competition. At a meeting of the board of directors of the Union Pacific Railroad in New York in 1871, called to decide which company would supply them with sleeping cars, he acted.

Mr. Pullman and myself were in attendance, both striving to obtain the prize which neither he nor I undervalued. One evening we began to mount the broad staircase in the St. Nicholas Hotel at the same time. We had met before, but were not well acquainted. I said, however, as we walked up the stairs:

"Good-evening, Mr. Pullman! Here we are together, and are we not making a nice couple of fools of ourselves?" He was not disposed to admit anything and said:

"What do you mean?"

I explained the situation to him. We were destroying by our rival propositions the very advantages we desired to obtain.

"Well," he said, "what do you propose to do about it?"

"Unite," I said. "Make a joint proposition to the Union Pacific, your party and mine, and organize a company."

"What would you call it?" he asked.

"The Pullman Palace Car Company," I replied.

This suited him exactly; and it suited me equally well.

"Come into my room and talk it over," said the great sleeping-car man.

I did so, and the result was that we obtained the contract jointly. Our company was subsequently merged in the general Pullman Company and we took stock in that company for our Pacific interests. Until compelled to sell my shares during the subsequent financial panic of 1873 to protect our iron and steel interests, I was, I believe, the largest shareholder in the Pullman Company.

Carnegie also believed in cultivating strong associates. He was good at finding competent men to work with and for him, and he kept them loyal by allowing them to share some of his earnings, even to the point that several of them became wealthy. The sharing, however, applied primarily to upper management, to men he believed possessed business and managerial skills. Ordinary laborers were different, and his treatment of them was both paternalistic and parsimonious. In 1903, when he was president of the British Iron and Steel Institute, he gave a speech to that organization entitled "The Human Side of Business." In the excerpt that follows (which appeared in his *Miscellaneous Writings*) he carefully avoided saying that the owner had an obligation to share profits with all who worked for him. Money was not the only way for the owner to show his appreciation to laborers.

I never see a fishing fleet set sail without pleasure, thinking this is based upon the form which is probably to prevail generally. Not a man in the boats is paid fixed wages. Each gets his share of the profits. That seems to me the idea. It would be most interesting if we could compare the results of a fleet so manned and operated with one in which men were paid fixed wages; but I question whether such a fleet as the latter exists. From my experience, I should say a crew of employees versus a crew of partners would not be in the race.

The great secret of success in business of all kinds, and especially in manufacturing, where a small saving in each process means fortune, is a liberal division of profits among the men who help to make them, and the wider distribution the better. Unsuspected powers lie latent in willing men around us which only need appreciation and development to produce surprising results. Money rewards alone will not, however, insure these, for to the most sensitive and ambitious natures there must be the note of sympathy, appreciation, friendship. Genius is sensitive in all its forms, and it is unusual, not ordinary, ability that tells even in practical affairs. You must capture and keep the heart of the original and supremely able man before his brain can do its best. Indeed this law has no limits. Even the mere laborer becomes more efficient as regard for his employer grows. Hand service or head service, it is heart service that counts.

One of the chief sources of whatever success may have attended the Carnegie Steel Company was undoubtedly its policy of making numerous partners from among the ablest of its men, and interesting so many others of ability in results. I strongly recommend this plan to the members of the Institute engaged in business, believing that in these days of ever-increasing competition it will be the concerns which adopt this plan, other things being equal, which will survive and flourish.

Disputes of some kind between capital and labor are always in evidence, but it must never be forgotten that in the wide fields of domestic service and in that of the few employees with a working master which combined embrace by far the greater number of wage-earners, all is, upon the whole, satisfactory; there reigns peace, with the inevitable individual exceptions.

We see in this encouraging fact the potent and salutary influence of the personal element. The employer knows his men and the men know their employer; there is mutual respect, sympathy, kindly interest and good feeling, hence peace. . . .The trusty servant becomes practically a member of the family, deeply attached to it, and the family reciprocates the feeling. Few householders are without old retainers and pensioners, and to the end of their days and even to that of the children of the household the relation remains unbroken. The friendship of the employers and their children for the old servants, and the affection of these for their masters and mistresses and their children, is one of the most delightful features of life.

What has produced this reciprocal affection? Not the mere payment of stipulated wages on the one part and the bare performance of stipulated duties on the other—far from this. It is the something more done upon both sides, and the knowledge each has had opportunity to gather of the other, their virtues, kindness—in short, their characters. The strict terms of the contract are drowned in the deep well of mutual regard. Labor is never fully paid by money alone.

If the managing owners and officials of great corporations could only be known to their men and, equally important, their men known to their employers, and the hearts of each exposed to the other, as well as their difficulties, we should have in that troublesome field such harmony as delights us in the domestic. It is mainly the ignorance of contending parties of each other's virtues that breeds quarrels everywhere throughout the world, between individuals, between corporations and their men—and between nations. "We only hate those we do not know" is a sound maxim which we do well ever to bear in mind.

Carnegie believed that everyone who worked for him loved him. Rightly or wrongly, he took the regard his workers showed him as a man of wealth and power to be true expressions of affection. He was convinced that he could charm men of any work level to follow his leadership. In times of crisis he often met with labor groups, and he always told labor representatives that despite being their boss he was one of them. Even after the tragic Homestead affair he visited the scene of the violence and came away certain that the workers there still trusted him. He believed that his success in business, as financier, producer, leader of working men, gave him the right to tell others how to be successful; and he gladly, freely gave advice to anyone who would listen. In a speech to the students at Curry Commercial College in Pittsburgh in 1885, he outlined what he called the "conditions essential to success." This was not a sermon, he felt the need to assure his audience, but merely the observations of "a man of the world, desirous of aiding the young men to become successful business men."

> You all know that there is no genuine, praiseworthy success in life if you are not honest, truthful, fair-dealing. I assume you are and will remain all these, and also that you are determined to live pure, respectable lives, free from pernicious or equivocal associations with one sex or the other. There is no creditable future for you else. Otherwise your learning and your advantages not only go for naught, but serve to accentuate your failure and your disgrace. I hope you will not take it amiss if I warn you against three of the gravest dangers which will beset you in your upward path.
>
> The first and most seductive, and the destroyer of most young men, is the drinking of liquor. [Carnegie is said to have drunk only moderately at meals.] I am no temperance lecturer in disguise, but a

man who knows and tells you what observation has proved to him; and I say to you that you are more likely to fail in your career from acquiring the habit of drinking liquor than from any, or all, the other temptations likely to assail you. You may yield to almost any other temptation and reform—may brace up, and if not recover lost ground, at least remain in the race and secure and maintain a respectable position. But from the insane thirst for liquor escape is almost impossible. I have known but few exceptions to this rule. First, then, you must not drink liquor to excess. Better if you do not touch it at all—much better; but if this be too hard a rule for you then take your stand firmly here:—Resolve never to touch it except at meals. A glass at dinner will not hinder your advance in life or lower your tone; but I implore you hold it inconsistent with the dignity and self-respect of gentlemen, with what is due from yourselves to your-selves, being the men you are, and especially the men you are determined to become, to drink a glass of liquor at a bar. Be far too much of the gentleman ever to enter a barroom. You do not pursue your careers in safety unless you stand firmly upon this ground. Adhere to it and you have escaped danger from the deadliest of your foes.

The next greatest danger to a young business man in this community I believe to be that of speculation. When I was a telegraph operator here we had no Exchanges in the City, but the men or firms who speculated upon the Eastern Exchanges were necessarily known to the operators. They could be counted on the fingers of one hand. These men were not our citizens of first repute; they were regarded with suspicion. I have lived to see all of these speculators irreparably ruined men, bankrupt in money and bankrupt in character. There is scarcely an instance of a man who has made a fortune by speculation and kept it. Gamesters die poor, and there is certainly not an instance of a speculator who has lived a life creditable to himself, or advantageous to the community. The man who grasps the morning paper to see first how his speculative ventures upon the Exchanges are likely to result, unfits himself for the calm consideration and proper solution of business problems, with which he has to deal later in the day, and saps the sources of that persistent and concentrated energy upon which depend the permanent success, and often the very safety, of his main business.

———

The third and last danger against which I shall warn you is one which has wrecked many a fair craft which started well and gave promise of a prosperous voyage. It is the perilous habit of indorsing—all the more dangerous, inasmuch as it assails one generally in the garb of friendship. It appeals to your generous instincts, and you say, "How can I refuse to lend my name only, to assist a friend?" It is because there is so much that is true and commendable in that view that the practice is so dangerous. Let me endeavor to put you upon safe honourable grounds in regard to it. I would say to you to make it a rule now, *never indorse*: but this is too much like never taste wine, or never smoke, or any other of the "nevers." They generally result in exceptions. You will as business men now and then probably become security for friends. Now, here is the line at which regard for the success of friends should cease and regard for your own honour begin.

I beseech you avoid liquor, speculation and indorsement. Do not fail in either, for liquor and speculation are the Scylla and Charybdis of the young man's business sea, and indorsement his rock ahead.

Despite his decisive investments, first in bridge building, then in steel manufacturing, Carnegie was at heart conservative. His earliest investments cost him relatively little in private outlay; he gradually consolidated his various investments into one; he sold off peripheral holdings to protect his major investment when it was threatened; and he never made speculative investments in companies which he did not himself run.

In his *Autobiography* he described how during the financial panic of 1873, just after he had entered the steel business, he sold other holdings to protect his primary company. By doing so, he explained, he both saved his steel company and earned the respect of the established businessmen of the country, thereby assuring him of their trust and support in the future. He contended that he was "compelled" to take over other men's interests in his steel plants when they could not make payments. He admitted no greed.

When the cyclone [financial panic] of 1873 struck us we at once began to reef sail in every quarter. Very reluctantly did we decide that the construction of the new steel works must cease for a time. Several prominent persons, who had invested in them, became unable to meet their payments and I was compelled to take over their interests, repaying the full cost to all. In that way control of the company came into my hands.

The first outburst of the storm had affected the financial world connected with the Stock Exchange. It was some time before it reached the commercial and manufacturing world. But the situation grew worse and worse and finally led to the crash which involved my friends in the Texas Pacific enterprise. . . .This was to me the severest blow of all. People could, with difficulty, believe that occupying such

intimate relations as I did with the Texas group I could by any possibility have kept myself clear of their financial obligations.

Mr. Schoenberger, president of the Exchange Bank at Pittsburgh,
with which we conducted a large business, was in New York when
the news reached him of the embarrassment of Mr. [Thomas A.]
Scott and Mr. [John Edgar] Thomson. He hastened to Pittsburgh, and
at a meeting of his board next morning said it was simply impossible that I was not involved with them. He suggested that the bank
should refuse to discount more of our bills receivable. He was
alarmed to find that the amount of these bearing our endorsement
and under discount, was so large. Prompt action on my part was
necessary to prevent serious trouble. I took the first train for
Pittsburgh, and was able to announce there to all concerned that,
although I was a shareholder in the Texas enterprise, my interest
was paid for. My name was not upon one dollar of their paper or of
any other outstanding paper. I stood clear and clean without a financial obligation or property which I did not own and which was not
fully paid for. My only obligations were those connected with our
business; and I was prepared to pledge for it every dollar I owned,
and to endorse every obligation the firm had outstanding.

Up to this time I had the reputation in business of being a bold,
fearless, and perhaps a somewhat reckless young man. Our operations had been extensive, our growth rapid and, although still
young, I had been handling millions. My own career was thought by
the elderly ones of Pittsburgh to have been rather more brilliant
than substantial. I know of an experienced one who declared that if
"Andrew Carnegie's brains did not carry him through his luck
would." But I think nothing could be farther from the truth than the
estimate thus suggested. I am sure that any competent judge would
be surprised to find how little I ever risked for myself or my partners. When I did big things, some large corporation like the
Pennsylvania Railroad Company was behind me and the responsible
party. My supply of Scotch caution never has been small; but I was
apparently something of a dare-devil now and then to the manufacturing fathers of Pittsburgh. They were old and I was young, which
made all the difference.

Carnegie's "Scotch caution" made him suspicious of stock speculation; and despite his early reputation as something of a "dare-devil," he
was actually quite careful how he conducted his business. He made the
following comments about speculation in that speech at Curry
Commercial College.

I have never bought or sold a share of stock speculatively in my life,
except one small lot of Pennsylvania Railroad shares that I bought

early in life for investment and for which I did not pay at the time because bankers offered to carry it for me at a low rate. I have adhered to the rule never to purchase what I did not pay for, and never to sell what I did not own. In those early days, however, I had several interests that were taken over in the course of business. They included some stocks and securities that were quoted on the New York Stock Exchange, and I found that when I opened my paper in the morning I was tempted to look first at the quotations of the stock market. As I had determined to sell all my interests in every outside concern and concentrate my attention upon our man-ufacturing concerns in Pittsburgh, I further resolved not even to own any stock that was bought and sold upon any stock exchange. With the exception of trifling amounts which came to me in various ways I have adhered strictly to this rule.

Such a course should commend itself to every man in the manu-facturing business and to all professional men. For the manufacturing man especially the rule would seem all-important. His mind must be kept calm and free if he is to decide wisely the problems which are continually coming before him. Nothing tells in the long run like good judgment, and no sound judgment can remain with the man whose mind is disturbed by the mercurial changes of the Stock Exchange. It places him under an influence akin to intoxication. What is not, he sees, and what he sees, is not. He cannot judge of rela-tive values or get the true perspective of things. The molehill seems to him a mountain and the mountain a molehill, and he jumps at con-clusions which he should arrive at by reason. His mind is upon the stock quotations and not upon the points that require calm thought. Speculation is a parasite feeding upon values, creating none.

In an article titled "How to Win a Fortune," published in the *New York Tribune* on April 18, 1890, Carnegie summed up his thoughts on economic success.

One great cause of failure of young men in business is lack of con-centration. They are prone to seek outside investments. The cause of many a surprising failure lies in so doing. Every dollar of capital and credit, every business thought, should be concentrated upon the one business upon which a man has embarked. He should never scatter his shot. It is a poor business which will not yield better returns for increased capital than any outside investment. No man or set of men or corporation can manage a business man's capital as well as he can manage it himself. The rule, "Do not put all your eggs in one basket," does not apply to a man's life work. Put all your eggs in one basket, and then watch that basket, is the true doctrine—the most valuable rule of all. While business of all kinds has gone and is still going rapidly into a few vast concerns, it is nevertheless demonstrated that genuine ability, interested in the profits, is not only valuable but indispensable to their successful operation. Through corporations whose shares are sold daily upon the market; through partnerships that find it necessary to interest their ablest workers; through merchants who can manage their vast enterprises successfully only by interesting exceptional ability; in every quarter of the business world, avenues greater in number, wider in extent, easier of access than ever before existed, stand open to the sober, frugal, energetic and able mechanic, to the scientifically educated youth, to the office boy and to the clerk—avenues through which they can reap greater successes than were ever before within the reach of these classes in the history of the world.

When, therefore, the young man, in any position or in any business, explains and complains that he has not opportunity to prove his ability and to rise to partnership, the old answer suffices:

> "The fault, dear Brutus, is not in our stars,
> But in ourselves, that we are underlings."

CARNEGIE'S IMPERIUM IN THE AMERICAN POPULAR IMAGINATION

Carnegie captured the American popular imagination more completely than any of the other nineteenth-century captains of industry. He was the prototypical man of wealth, power, and influence, the kind of man ordinary Americans wanted to be. As an enormously rich man, one who influenced financial and public affairs, he exemplified the American spirit. He was indeed an icon.

ELIHU ROOT'S ADMIRATION

The respected statesman Elihu Root articulated this popular opinion of Carnegie in a speech before the Authors' Club of New York on April 15, 1920, soon after Carnegie's death. Having served as Secretary of War under Presidents McKinley and Roosevelt and Secretary of State under President Roosevelt, Root was himself one of the most admired men of his day, and his assessment of men in public life both reflected public opinion and molded it.

> He belonged to that great race of nation-builders who have made
> the progress and development of America the wonder of the world;
> who have exhibited the capacity of free, undominated, individual

genius for building up the highest example of the possibilities of freedom for nation.

Mr. Carnegie in amassing his fortune always gave more than he gained. His money was not taken from others. His money was the by-product of great constructive ability which served others; which contributed to the great business enterprises that he conceived and built up and carried to success, and through those enterprises gave to the world great advance in comfort and the possibilities of broader and happier life. The steps by which mankind proceeds from naked savagery to civilized society are the steps that are taken by just such constructive geniuses.

When Mr. Carnegie had amassed his fortune, the magnitude of which rested upon the introduction into America of the Bessemer method of making steel, with all the advance and the progress that that means; when Mr. Carnegie had amassed his fortune and had come to the point of retiring from money-making enterprise, it was impossible for him to retire. His nature made it impossible that he should become passive and he turned his constructive genius and the great constructive energy that urged him on, by the necessities of his nature, toward the use of the money which he had amassed.

Thus spoke one successful, admired American about another. Root's accomplishments were in diplomacy, Carnegie's in finance, but in the public mind they represented two sides of a coin.

UNQUESTIONING ADMIRATION

Root's comments reflected the wide admiration accorded Carnegie during the great days of his industrial triumph and subsequent philanthropic endeavors. From the 1880s until well after his death, a plethora of magazine articles and books praising his accomplishments were published and eagerly read by large audiences. Typical of such treatments is the following article published in *Cosmopolitan* in 1902, written just after Carnegie sold his empire, when he was considered the greatest of nineteenth-century industrialists. It is evident from the format that writer Charles S. Gleed and the magazine's editors considered Carnegie a giant. The article "Andrew Carnegie" was one in a series titled "Captains of Industry" about the great men of the age. Alongside one page of text ran a drawing of a woman, very much like the figure "Liberty" in many contemporary patriotic paintings, holding sway over a smoky factory that produced coins that in turn became books. At this time, Carnegie's grants were primarily to build libraries. He had not yet begun his wider philanthropic endeavors. Along another page ran an accountant's desk from which grew vines and branches leading up to

Drawings for the Cosmopolitan profile of Carnegie, showing how a poor boy-turned-millionaire had turned industry into money for libraries.

a goddess holding a crown of glory, doubtless meant for Carnegie's head. Just as the Scotsman would have done himself, Gleed made Carnegie the central figure in a tale of romance.

> All the people, in a general way, know about Mr. Carnegie; but how few really grasp the fairy-tale in all its fullness! It extinguishes the glory of Croesus and makes the story of Aladdin seem cheap. Think of historic old Fifeshire, Scotland, composed of equal parts of rocks and water—where the sea sends an arm into almost every estate and where brains are the biggest crop—Fifeshire, town of Dunfermline, 1837 [sic], that is where and when this favorite of fortune began his career. He began as poor as any little Scot who ever throve on sea air and oatmeal. And now what? The name which above all others will soon be found "blown in the bottle" in the United States is that of Carnegie—and the same Carnegie who began so humbly in Dunfermline sixty-five years ago. George Washington and Christopher Columbus will continue to be very well-known persons. States, cities, streets, institutions and cigars have been named for them and they have seemed almost beyond the reach of rivals in the same line. But now these great names are doomed to comparative disuse. They are to be distanced by the name "Carnegie." In a few years this name will be presented to the eye and ear of the people of the United States a thousand times where the others are once . . .

Gleed, in words appropriate to a romantic novel, described the people of Fife as hard-headed and thrifty, calculating and managerial. Carnegie's father was, according to Gleed's romance, a master-weaver with an exceptional intellect, his mother a woman with the courage and foresight of a natural financier. They brought Andrew to America in 1848 because the Old World offered too few opportunities for his talents, and rapidly he moved up the ladder from bobbin-boy to courier to telegraph operator to railroad manager and finally to industrialist. He sought challenges and met each one with skills that led inevitably to victory. He became, indeed, a Captain of Industry.

> He acquired various other manufacturing plants in the iron line. He always won. By 1888 he had control of the Homestead steel works, the Edgar Thompson steel works, the Upper Union rolling-mills and the Lower Union rolling-mills. These works were capitalized at about one hundred million dollars, the ownership including a vast amount of coal and iron lands. These properties were last year turned over to the United States Steel Corporation for two or three hundred millions of dollars in cash, first-mortgage bonds, and stock.
>
> Ten or fifteen years ago, Mr. Carnegie began to admit the oppression of his wealth and its responsibilities. He first made sundry

arrangements by which many of his employees became sharers in his profits—virtually partners.

After getting free of the greater part of the personal care of the properties in which he was chief owner, Mr. Carnegie devoted himself largely to two tasks—giving away his money and writing for publication.

His gifts have been chiefly in the line of building libraries. His greatest single gift was ten millions given to the trustees of the government for aid to the universities of the country. The particulars of this gift need not be recited. In all his work of giving Mr. Carnegie has remained, as in the beginning, a "canny Scot." While giving away millions, he will step aside to do a little business and—make millions. In the very business of giving away money he is as careful of how he does it, and as adherent to his own plans and policies, as if he were trying to get money instead of give it; and woe to those beggars who try to be choosers. There is not joy for those who try to tell him what he ought to do with his money. He will have his own way or no way. It has often been asked how Mr. Carnegie came to turn his chief charities in the direction of literary work. So practical a man, it is supposed, would have taken naturally to the more practical charities—hospitals, industrial schools, and the like. Probably the explanation is complex. His parents were book lovers. He was born with the same taste. He began very early to read with enthusiasm and purpose. While he was yet a bobbin-boy, with perhaps no book at home but the Bible, a gentleman who was on the lookout for chances to be helpful, Colonel John B. Anderson, arranged to supply him with all the books he could read. Colonel Anderson lived many years in Kansas, where he died. Mr. Carnegie never forgot his early kindness, and has given a pipe organ, a library and a statue of Colonel Anderson to Kansas institutions of which the latter was trustee. It is said that this early encouragement to give his spare time to good books instead of to bad companions has always been assigned by Mr. Carnegie as one of the explanations of why he has prospered and is therefore the kind of aid which he most prefers to pass on to the youth of the land.

Next to books, Mr. Carnegie's taste runs to music. His ancestors, or many of them, no doubt made war on fiddles and other musical instruments as encouraging ungodliness. But Mr. Carnegie has swung to the other side and has devoted millions to musical organizations and institutions.

It is natural for Mr. Carnegie to be a writer. He began doing odd bits of newspaper work when he was a telegraph operator. From that time to this he has been a frequent contributor to the publications of the country. His magazine articles and books are in every respect worth reading. The style in which they are written is excellent. It is characterized by plain words, crisp sentences and exceptionally lucid construction. The work of Mr. Carnegie's pen is worth reading, not because he is an exceptional philosopher nor because he is brilliant or profound more than others, but because there is always, in what he writes, something important out of his actual experience or knowledge as a practical man. There is never anything in what he writes (so far as I have been able to see) which suggests the idea of an audacious rich man attempting literary work as a fad. Though often wrong (as it seems to me), he is always respectably strong in the positions he takes and defends. He is optimistic, patriotic and conservative. He "stands up for poverty" in the most approved style of the rich man's art.

Mr. Carnegie is an optimist. "The 'good old times' were not good old times. Neither master nor servant was as well situated as to-day. What were the luxuries have become the necessities of life."

Mr. Carnegie often expresses his belief in the organization of labor, in improved hours of work, in bettered conditions for workmen, in subdued and regulated officialism—in short, in about all the things contended for by champions of labor. But, on the other hand, he smites with fury the socialists and communists who demand one level for all men. He says: "Civilization took its start from the day when the capable, industrious workman said to his incompetent and lazy fellow, 'If thou dost not sow, thou shalt not reap,' and thus ended primitive communism by separating the drones from the bees. One who studies this subject will soon be brought face to face with the conclusion that upon the sacredness of property civilization itself depends—the right of the laborer to his hundred dollars in the savings-bank, and equally the right of the millionaire to his millions."

While Mr. Carnegie thus vigorously defends the right of some people to have millions, he attacks with no less vigor the usual method of millionaires in applying what they have accumulated. He thinks great fortunes should be given back to the people in some systematic manner and in accordance with some wise plan. He thinks this is the only way for great and enduring advantages to reach the people; and he thinks the only way to do this properly is, not by will, but by an intelligent personal administration by the giver. "It is well to remember that it requires the exercise of not less ability than that which acquires it so as to be really beneficial to the community. . . .The growing disposition to tax more and more heavily the estates left at death is a cheering indication of the growth of a salutary change in public opinion."

It is not to be supposed that all men who are fit to be kings are crowned, nor that all men who are crowned are fit to be kings. It is not to be supposed that all men who are fit to be rich are rich, nor that all who are rich are fit to be so. Luck, or something wrongfully called luck, enters in and gives some men money who ought to be poor. A vote of all the people would undoubtedly decide, almost unanimously, that Andrew Carnegie is fit to be rich.

THE AMERICAN BUSINESSMAN AS CHRIST FIGURE

With such adoration for Carnegie wafting on the American air, with Carnegie-type industrialists and businessmen held in such high esteem, it is not surprising that someone would take the hyperbole one step farther, a giant step to be sure, and compare the modern businessman to Christ. Fifty years after Carnegie began to amass his wealth, twenty-five after he became the richest man in the world and retired to pursue philanthropic projects, the time came for this leap, and Bruce Barton made it. Barton captured the spirit of the Age of Carnegie, which after setbacks in the Progressive Age had revived and spilled over into his own time, the 1920s, in his best-selling book *The Man Nobody Knows*.

Barton described Jesus as the founder of modern American business: the prototype of the successful industrial executive; the teacher who could show modern managers how to select and train men, advertise, and develop a corporation that could conquer the world of industry and finance. In the process Barton sanctified business and businessmen. His book, appearing as it did in the Jazz Age, a time of unexcelled and apparently unlimited financial expansion, both reflected and enhanced the religious image of Carnegie and his fellow captains of industry, adding to the iconography of the day. He did not have to use specific names for readers to know he was describing men like Carnegie.

In his introduction, Barton explained how as a young man he had despised the weak, effeminate Jesus portrayed in Sunday sermons. It was not until he was a grown man, indeed a *business*man, long since having forsaken the traditional church, that he began to question that image. He spoke of himself in third person.

> He said to himself: "Only strong magnetic men inspire great enthusiasm and build great organizations. Yet Jesus built the greatest organization of all. It is extraordinary."
> The more sermons the man heard and the more books he read the more mystified he became.
> One day he decided to wipe his mind clean of books and sermons.

He said, "I will read what the men who knew Jesus personally said about him. I will read about him as though he were a new historical character, about whom I had never heard anything at all."

The man was amazed.

A physical weakling! Where did they get that idea? Jesus pushed a plane and swung an adze; he was a successful carpenter. He slept outdoors and spent his days walking around his favorite lake. His muscles were so strong that when he drove the money-changers out, nobody dared to oppose him!

A kill-joy! He was the most popular dinner guest in Jerusalem! The criticism which proper people made was that he spent too much time with publicans and sinners (very good fellows, on the whole, the man thought) and enjoyed society too much. They called him a "wine bibber and a gluttonous man."

A failure! He picked up twelve men from the bottom ranks of business and forged them into an organization that conquered the world.

When the man had finished his reading he exclaimed, "This is a man nobody knows."

"Some day," said he, "some one will write a book about Jesus. Every business man will read it and send it to his partners and his salesmen. For it will tell the story of the founder of modern business."

Barton said he waited in vain for someone to write that book. Meanwhile he heard more misinformed sermons about Jesus, the weak, unhappy man who was only too glad to die. At last he decided to write the book himself. *The Man Nobody Knows* was indeed read by businessmen, and many other people too, and they passed it around. Jesus became known to its readers as the father of modern business, and modern businessmen came to be regarded either as Christ figures or as exemplars of Christian enterprise. The following passage was Barton's description of Jesus as the prototype of the modern business executive.

In any crowd and under any circumstances the leader stands out. By the power of his faith in himself he commands, and men instinctively obey.

This blazing conviction was the first and greatest element in the success of Jesus. The second was his wonderful power to pick men, and to recognize hidden capacities in them. It must have amazed Nicodemus when he learned the names of the twelve whom the young teacher had chosen to be his associates. What a list! Not a single well-known person on it. Nobody who had ever made a success of anything. A haphazard collection of fishermen and small-town business men, and one tax collector—a member of the most hated element in the community. What a crowd!

———

He had the born leader's gift for seeing powers in men of which they themselves were often almost unconscious. One day as he was coming into a certain town a tremendous crowd pressed around him. There was a rich man named Zacchaeus in the town; small in stature, but with such keen business ability that he had got himself generally disliked. Being curious to see the distinguished visitor he had climbed up into a tree. Imagine his surprise when Jesus stopped under the tree and commanded him to come down saying, "To-day I intend to eat at your house." The crowd was stunned. Some of the bolder spirits took it upon themselves to tell Jesus of his social blunder. He couldn't afford to make the mistake of visiting Zacchaeus, they said. Their protests were without avail. They saw in Zacchaeus merely a dishonest little Jew; he saw in him a man of unusual generosity and a fine sense of justice, who needed only to have those qualities revealed by some one who understood. So with Matthew—the crowd saw only a despised tax-gatherer. Jesus saw the potential writer of a book that will live forever.

———

Having gathered together his organization, there remained for Jesus the tremendous task of training it. And herein lay the third great element in his success—his vast unending patience. The Church has attached to each of the disciples the title of Saint and thereby done most to destroy the conviction of their reality. They were very far from sainthood when he picked them up. For three years he had them with him day and night, his whole energy and resources poured out in an effort to create an understanding in them.

———

He had only twelve, and they were untrained simple men, with elementary weakness and passions. Yet because of the fire of his personal conviction, because of his marvelous instinct for discovering their latent powers, and because of his unwavering faith and patience, he molded them into an organization which carried on victoriously. Within a very few years after his death, it was reported in a far-off corner of the Roman Empire that "these who have turned the world upside down have come hither also." A few decades later the proud Emperor himself bowed his head to the teachings of this Nazareth carpenter, transmitted through common men.

Barton also showed how Jesus demonstrated the principles upon which successful advertising is based. "Every advertising man ought to study the parables of Jesus," he said. They were "marvelously condensed," the language "marvelously simple," hardly ever qualified and never complicated. "Sincerity glistened like sunshine through every sentence he uttered," Barton said, the kind of sincerity necessary for good marketing; and Jesus understood the importance of "repetition" in order to drive home the advertiser's message. "Because the advertisements were unforgettable, the Idea lived," he concluded, "and is to-day the one most powerful influence on human action and thought."

Barton found the essence of Jesus' gospel of business in the story of how his parents found him in the temple when he was twelve years of age.

> . . . but what interests us most in this one recorded incident of his boyhood is the fact that for the first time he defined the purpose of his career. He did not say, "Wist ye not that I must practise preaching?" or "Wist ye not that I must get ready to meet the arguments of men like these?" The language was quite different, and well worth remembering. "Wist ye not that I must be about my father's *business?*" he said. He thought of his life as *business.* What did he mean by business? To what extent are the principles by which he conducted his business applicable to ours? And if he were among us again, in our highly competitive world, would his business philosophically work?
>
> On one occasion, you recall, he stated his recipe for success. It was on the afternoon when James and John came to ask him what promotion they might expect . . . "Master," they said, "we want to ask what plans you have in mind for us. You're going to need big men around you when you establish your kingdom; our ambition is to sit on either side of you, one on the right hand and the other on the left."
>
> Who can object to that attitude? If a man fails to look after himself, certainly no one will look after him. If you want a big place, go ask for it. That's the way to get ahead.
>
> Jesus answered with a sentence which sounds poetically absurd.
>
> "Whosoever will be great among you, shall be your minister," he said, "and whosoever of you will be the chiefest, shall be servant of all."
>
> A fine piece of rhetoric, now isn't it? Be a good servant and you will be great; be the best possible servant and you will occupy the highest possible place. Nice idealistic talk but utterly impractical; nothing to take seriously in a common sense world. That is just what men thought for some hundreds of years; and then, quite suddenly, Business woke up to a great discovery. You will hear that discovery proclaimed in every sales convention as something distinctly modern and up to date. It is emblazoned in the advertising pages of every magazine.
>
> Look through those pages.

> Here is the advertisement of an automobile company, one of the greatest in the world. And why is it greatest? On what does it base its claim to leadership? On its huge factories and financial strength? They are never mentioned. On its army of workmen or its high salaried executives? You might read its advertisements for years without suspecting that it had either. No. "We are great because of our service," the advertisements cry. "We will crawl under your car oftener and get our backs dirtier than any of our competitors. Drive up to our service station and ask for anything at all—it will be granted cheerfully. We serve; therefore we grow."

Barton went on to delineate other business principles Jesus preached, all of them for centuries thought to be only religious in nature, but which Barton hoped would be recognized by the world of business as keys to financial and industrial success.

> "Try to save your life, and you will lose it; lose it, and you will find it." Businessmen have discovered that if they give their whole selves to their work, losing their lives to their industry, they will emerge "bigger and richer than they ever supposed they could be." He who starts out only to make money will never make any; but he who sets out to perfect a product will find himself rich.
> "If a man compels you to go with him a mile, go with him twain." Businessmen have learned that if they give twice the service they are asked to give, they will harvest much more than twice the profits.
> "It is more blessed to give than to receive." Businessmen have learned, along with Jesus and Ralph Waldo Emerson, that the "great unselfish soul forgets himself into immortality."

Barton's "Christ as Businessman" may seem extreme; but the popularity of *The Man Nobody Knows* proved that in the 1920s the American tycoon was still the most admired figure on the American scene, worthy to be compared with Christ.

Yet this admiration was by no means universal, and the positive image of American industrialists did not go unchallenged. Detractors began their criticism as far back as the 1870s, when Carnegie was just beginning his climb to wealth; and they continued to condemn industrialists and to call for curbs on the unbridled accumulation of money and power-especially at the expense of the men who worked for them—well into the twentieth century.

Among the detractors was author Henry Demarest Lloyd, who analyzed America's industrial revolution, its leaders, its effects on the American public, in his great work *Wealth Against Commonwealth*. Lloyd began with a paraphrase of Jean-Jacques Rousseau's famous opening statement in *On The Social Contract:* "Man was born free, and everywhere he is in chains." America in the last years of the nineteenth century, Lloyd said, reflected a similar reality: "Nature is rich; but everywhere man, the heir of nature, is poor." He blamed this depressing fact on men like Carnegie, who had "cornered" markets and made fortunes by selling the riches of the earth, which should belong to everyone. "The world, enriched by thousands of generations of toilers and thinkers, has reached a fertility which can give every human being a plenty undreamed of even in the Utopias. But between this plenty ripening on the boughs of our civilization and the people hungering for it step the 'cornerers'. . . ."

Lloyd made an indelible imprint on American thought. He demonstrated to his readers that the third leg of Carnegie's stool, labor, was being starved out of the great industrial feast. American businessmen exhibited little of Jesus' compassion for the poor and weak.

LITERARY CHALLENGE TO THE IMAGE: EDWARD BELLAMY

Lloyd was not alone in his criticism. Seven years before the publication of *Wealth and Commonwealth,* Edward Bellamy published his novel *Looking Backward.* Bellamy told the story of a man named Julian West, who fell into a deep sleep in 1887 and awoke in the marvelous year 2000, when America had built a system of comprehensive economic prosperity, equality, and justice. Although Bellamy spent most of his story describing that wonderful world (which, incidentally, did not have automobiles or television), he did have West describe to people of the twentieth century what things were like back in the bad old days of the nineteenth. People who read this novel in 1887—and it too was a bestseller—were left in no doubt that Bellamy considered the system of his day desperately unjust.

> Perhaps I cannot do better than to compare society as it was then to a prodigious coach which the masses of humanity were harnessed to and dragged toilsomely along a very hilly and sandy road. The driver was hunger, and permitted no lagging, though the pace was necessarily very slow. Despite the difficulty of drawing the coach at all along so hard a road, the top was covered with passengers who never got down, even at the steepest ascents. These seats on top were very breezy and comfortable. Well up out of the dust, their occupants could enjoy the scenery at their leisure, or critically discuss the merits of the straining team. Naturally such places were in great demand and the competition for them was keen, every one seeking as the first end in life to secure a seat on the coach for himself and to leave it to his child after him. By the rule of the coach a man could leave his seat to whom he wished, but on the other hand

there were so many accidents by which it might at any time be
wholly lost. For all that they were so easy, the seats were very inse-
cure, and at every sudden jolt of the coach persons were slipping
out of them and falling to the ground, where they were instantly
compelled to take hold of the rope and help to drag the coach on
which they had before ridden so pleasantly. It was naturally regarded
as a terrible misfortune to lose one's seat, and the apprehension that
this might happen to them or their friends was a constant cloud
upon the happiness of those who rode.

But did they think only of themselves? you ask. Was not their
very luxury rendered intolerable to them by comparison with the
lot of their brothers and sisters in the harness, and the knowledge
that their own weight added to their toil? Had they no compassion
for fellow beings from whom fortune only distinguished them? Oh,
yes, commiseration was frequently expressed by those who rode for
those who had to pull the coach, especially when the vehicle came
to a bad place in the road, as it was constantly doing, or to a particularly steep hill. At such times, the desperate straining of the team,
their agonized leaping and plunging under the pitiless lashing of
hunger, the many who fainted at the rope and were trampled in the
mire, made a very distressing spectacle, which often called forth
highly creditable displays of feeling on the top of the coach. At such
times the passengers would call down encouragingly to the toilers
of the rope, exhorting them to patience, and holding out hopes of
possible compensation in another world for the hardness of their
lot, while others contributed to buy salves and liniments for the
crippled and injured. It was agreed that it was a great pity that the
coach should be so hard to pull, and there was a sense of general
relief when the specially bad piece of road was gotten over. This
relief was not, indeed, wholly on account of the team, for there was
always some danger at these bad places of a general overturn in
which all would lose their seats.

It must in truth be admitted that the main effect of the spectacle
of the misery of the toilers at the rope was to enhance the passengers' sense of the value of their seats upon the coach, and to cause
them to hold on to them more desperately than before. If the passengers could only have felt assured that neither they nor their friends
would ever fall from the top, it is probable that, beyond contributing
to the funds for liniments and bandages, they would have troubled
themselves extremely little about those who dragged the coach.

I am well aware that this will appear to the men and women of
the twentieth century an incredible inhumanity, but there are two
facts, both very curious, which partly explain it. In the first place, it
was firmly and sincerely believed that there was no other way in
which Society could get along, except the many pulled at the rope

and the few rode, and not only this, but that no very radical
improvement even was possible, either in the harness, the coach,
the roadway, or the distribution of the toil. It had always been as it
was, and it always would be so. It was a pity, but it could not be
helped, and philosophy forbade wasting compassion on what was
beyond remedy.

The other fact is yet more curious, consisting in a singular hallucination which those on the top of the coach generally shared, that
they were not exactly like their brothers and sisters who pulled at
the rope, but of finer clay, in some way belonging to a higher order
of beings who might justly expect to be drawn. This seems unac-
countable, but, as I once rode on this very coach and shared that
very hallucination, I ought to be believed. The strangest thing about
the hallucination was that those who had but just climbed up from
the ground, before they had outgrown the marks of the rope upon
their hands, began to fall under its influence. As for those whose
parents and grandparents before them had been so fortunate as to
keep their seats on the top, the conviction they cherished of the
essential difference between their sort of humanity and the common article was absolute. The effect of such a delusion in moderat-
ing fellow feeling for the sufferings of the mass of men into a distant
and philosophical compassion is obvious. To it I refer as the only
extenuation I can offer for the indifference which, at the period I
write of, marked by own attitude toward the misery of my brothers.

Mr. West's host in the year 2000 was a Dr. Leete, who explained
to him how the America of 2000 came to be, how the American system was transformed into the utopia West saw around him. In one
conversation West and Leete discussed the way wealth came to be
unwholesomely concentrated in the hands of a few rich men and
how working men had no alternative but to take industrial action.
Some modern economists take issue with Bellamy's analysis of the
nineteenth-century labor movement; but this is how the nineteenth-
century novelist saw things.

Before this concentration began, while as yet commerce and industry were conducted by innumerable petty concerns with small capital, instead of a small number of great concerns with vast capital, the
individual workman was relatively important and independent in his
relations to the employer. Moreover, when a little capital or a new
idea was enough to start a man in business for himself, workingmen
were constantly becoming employers and there was no hard and
fast line between the two classes. Labor unions were needless then,
and general strikes out of the question. But when the era of small
concerns with small capital was succeeded by that of the great

aggregations of capital, all this was changed. The individual laborer, who had been relatively important to the small employer, was reduced to insignificance and powerlessness over against the great corporation, while at the same time the way upward to the grade of employer was closed to him. Self-defense drove him to union with his fellows.

The records of the period show that the outcry against the concentration of capital was furious. Men believed that it threatened society with a form of tyranny more abhorrent than it had ever endured. They believed that the great corporations were preparing for them the yoke of a baser servitude than had ever been imposed on the race, servitude not to men but to soulless machines incapable of any motive but insatiable greed. Looking back, we cannot wonder at their desperation, for certainly humanity was never confronted with a fate more sordid and hideous than would have been the era of corporate tyranny which they anticipated.

Meanwhile, without being in the smallest degree checked by the clamor against it, the absorption of business by ever larger monopolies continued. . . .

POLITICAL CHALLENGE FROM THE POPULISTS: IGNATIUS DONNELLY

In the 1880s, while a few writers excoriated the captains of industry, a new political movement arose in the west to challenge the two established parties. The People's Party, or Populists, were primarily Midwestern farmers and Rocky Mountain miners, and their beef was against the railroads which charged such high prices to take crops to markets and the Eastern bankers who controlled the currency and favored gold over Western silver. As earlier noted, Populist orators were the first people to employ the term robber barons for their enemies, naming them after the landed aristocrats of the late Middle Ages who preyed on travelers passing their fortified castles. At first this term referred primarily to railroad and banking tycoons, but it soon expanded to include industrialists. They were the "bad guys" of Populist political theater. When in 1934 Matthew Josephson published his famous study of the captains of industry, he naturally titled it *The Robber Barons*.

By 1892, with neither Republicans nor Democrats responsive to their complaints and proposed reforms, the Populists ran James B. Weaver for President and captured over a million votes, nearly ten percent of the popular tally, and twenty-two electoral votes. Unfortunately for them this was the high water mark of their electoral history, but for a brief moment they smelled the heady scent of future victory. When they met in Omaha, Nebraska, in July of 1892 to nominate Weaver, they adopted a revolutionary platform aimed at curbing the excesses of the fabulously rich industrialists and giving the profits of labor to the working classes. The preamble to their platform, written by Ignatius Donnelly, was a classic contemporary statement of disdain for the economic abuses of the Carnegie Era.

The conditions which surround us best justify our cooperation: we meet in the midst of a nation brought to the verge of moral, political, and material ruin. Corruption dominates the ballot-box, the legislatures, the Congress, and touches even the ermine of the bench. The people are demoralized; most of the States have been compelled to isolate the voters at the polling-places to prevent universal intimidation or bribery. The newspapers are largely subsidized or muzzled; public opinion silenced; business prostrated; our homes covered with mortgages; labor impoverished; and the land concentrating in the hands of the capitalists. The urban workmen are denied the right of organization for self-protection; imported pauperized labor beats down their wages; a hireling standing army, unrecognized by our laws, is established to shoot them down, and they are rapidly degenerating into European conditions. The fruits of the toil of millions are boldly stolen to build up colossal fortunes for a few, unprecedented in the history of mankind; and the possessors of these, in turn, despise the republic and endanger liberty. From the same prolific womb of governmental injustice we breed the two great classes-tramps and millionaires.

The national power to create money is appropriated to enrich bondholders; a vast public debt, payable in legal tender currency, has been funded into gold-bearing bonds, thereby adding millions to the burdens of the people. Silver, which has been accepted as coin since the dawn of history, has been demonetized to add to the purchasing power of gold by decreasing the value of all forms of property as well as human labor; and the supply of currency is purposely abridged to fatten usurers, bankrupt enterprise, and enslave industry. A vast conspiracy against mankind has been organized on two continents, and it is rapidly taking possession of the world. If not met and overthrown at once, it forebodes terrible social convulsions, the destruction of civilization, or the establishment of an absolute despotism.

We have witnessed for more than a quarter of a century the struggles of the two great political parties for power and plunder, while grievous wrongs have been inflicted upon the suffering people. We charge that the controlling influences dominating both these parties have permitted the existing dreadful conditions to develop without serious effort to prevent or restrain them. Neither do they now promise us any substantial reform. They have agreed together to ignore in the coming campaign every issue but one. They propose to drown the outcries of a plundered people with the uproar of a sham battle over the tariff, so that capitalists, corporations, national banks, rings, trusts, watered stock, the demonetization of silver, and the oppressions of the usurers may be lost sight of. They propose to sacrifice our homes, lives and children on the altar of mammon; to destroy the multitude in order to secure corruption funds from the millionaires.

The People's Party never controlled Congress and never elected a President. They were unwilling or unable to expand their base of farmers and miners to include the urban labor force, even though they tried to speak for factory workers when they labeled the industrial merchants robber barons. The interests of urban-industrial workers were simply different from those of the agrarian Populists. In 1896, when the Democrats nominated the young Nebraskan William Jennings Bryan for president and in his acceptance speech he spoke in support of "Populist" causes, the People's Party nominated him too; and in doing so they lost their identity. They never again fielded a presidential candidate. On the other hand, Populist ideas—criticism of big industry and business, condemnation of monopolies, calls for economic and social reform, demands that power be taken from plutocracies and given to the common man—took root in both the major parties.

The term more commonly used to describe Democrats and Republicans who came to espouse Populist and other major systematic political and economic reforms was "Progressive." Between 1900 and 1920 the most dynamic leaders of both parties identified themselves that way. There is no direct historical link between the Populist Party and the Progressives of both major parties or the Progressive Party that nominated Theodore Roosevelt in 1912 and Robert LaFollette in 1924. Indeed most Progressives would have denied any direct connection. But Progressives did carry on a number of Populist causes, including the breakup of monopolies.

By the turn of the twentieth century, in order to avoid legislation against monopolies, the big companies had created "trusts," holding boards that allowed them to continue their monopolistic ways. Progressives also challenged these "trusts," which they believed were still holding the nation, its people, and its economy hostage to unfair practices. They were not, as popular history says, "trustbusters" to any great degree; but they did oppose the abuses of corporate American business, and they used the threat of governmental intervention to curb some of these abuses.

PROGRESSIVE CHALLENGE:
LOUIS BRANDEIS'S "COMPETITION"

Republican Theodore Roosevelt (1901–1909) was the first Progressive president, and during his second term, he began the job of trying to control big business. Four years after he left office, the Democrats elected a Progressive president, Woodrow Wilson (1913–1921); and Wilson's first two years as president saw major economic reform. Like his predecessor Roosevelt, Wilson sought to "control" the abuses of the big corporations. Advising him during this period was the scholarly, outspoken lawyer Louis D. Brandeis. In 1916, Wilson named Brandeis to the Supreme Court.

In the following article published in *American Legal News* in 1913, just as the Wilsonian reforms were being enacted, Brandeis argued that large industrial and manufacturing combinations should be curtailed and controlled so that the American economy could be competitive. Competition, assured through governmental action, was the key to greater opportunity, greater equality, and not the least greater efficiency.

> Regulation is essential to the preservation of competition and to its best development just as regulation is necessary to the preservation and development of civil or political liberty. To serve civil and political liberty to the many we have found it necessary to restrict the liberty of the few. Unlicensed liberty leads necessarily to despotism or oligarchy. Those who are stronger must to some extent be curbed. We curb the physically strong in order to protect those physically weaker. . . .
>
> The right of competition must be similarly limited; for excesses of competition lead to monopoly just as excesses of liberty have led to despotism. It is another case where the extremes meet.

> . . . .We may emphatically declare: "Give fair play to efficiency."
>
> One has heard of late the phrases: "You can't make people compete by law." "Artificial competition is undesirable." These are truisms, but their implication is false. Believers in competition make no suggestion that traders be compelled to compete. They ask merely that no trader should be allowed to kill competition. Competition consists in trying to do things better than someone else; that is, making or selling a better article, or the same article at a lesser cost, or otherwise giving better service. It is not competition to resort to methods of the prize ring, and simply "knock the other man out." That is killing a competitor. . . .

Earnest argument is constantly made in support of monopoly by pointing to the wastefulness of competition. Undoubtedly competition involves some waste. What human activity does not? The wastes of democracy are among the greatest obvious wastes, but we have compensations in democracy which far outweigh that waste and make it more efficient than absolutism. So it is with competition. Incentive and development which are incident to the former system of business result in so much achievement that the accompanying waste is relatively insignificant. The margin between that which men naturally do and which they can do is so great that a system which urges men on to action, enterprise, and initiative is preferable in spite of the wastes that necessarily attend that process. . . .

But the efficiency of monopolies, even if established, would not justify their existence unless the community should reap benefit from the efficiency; experience teaches us that whenever trusts have developed efficiency, their fruits have been absorbed almost wholly by the trusts themselves. From such efficiency as they have developed the community has gained substantially nothing. . . .

Diagnosis shows monopoly to be an artificial, not a natural, product. Competition, therefore, may be preserved by preventing that course of conduct by which in the past monopolies have been established. If we had in the past undertaken by appropriate legal and administrative machinery to prevent our financiers and others from carrying out agreements to form monopolies; if we had seriously attempted to prevent those methods of destructive or unfair competition, as are manifest in "cut-throat competition"—discrimination against customers who will not deal exclusively with the combination; if we had made any persistent, intelligent effort to stop advantages gained by railroad discrimination, espionage, or the practice of establishing "fake dependents," or to stop those who have secured control of essential raw material from denying business rivals access to it—few of the trusts, of which we now complain, would have come into existence, or would, at all events, have acquired power to control the market. We made no serious attempt to stop monopoly—certainly no intelligent attempt; partly because we lacked knowledge, partly because we lacked desire; for we had a sneaking feeling that perhaps, after all, a private monopoly might be a good thing, and we had no adequate governmental machinery to employ for this purpose. But in the past twenty-two years we have acquired much experience with trusts. We know their ways. We have learned what the defects in the existing machinery are; and if we will but remedy those defects by appropriate legal and administrative machinery . . . And supplement the prohibition of monopoly by the regulation of competition, we shall be able, not only to preserve the competition we now enjoy, but gradually regain the free soil upon which private monopoly has encroached, and we may be assured that, despite all industrial changes, the day for industrial liberty has not yet passed.

Carnegie sold his empire before the Progressives had much effect on the American economy. Although he was retired by the time Roosevelt and Wilson were in the White House, it was his form of economic imperialism that they believed they needed to control for the national good.

ROBERT HEILBRONER AND JOSEPH WALL EVALUATE CARNEGIE AS TYCOON

The Carnegies of the turn of the twentieth century were controversial men in their own day, and they still are today. To some they were icons of the American dream, while to others they were exploiters of their fellow men. They were Christ figures or they were greedy monopolists. They were, and they still are, both loved and admired, hated and despised.

Scholars, however, try to look at them with as much detachment and objectivity as possible. Difficult as this may be to do, the passage of time does help clear the air of emotion and provide a better view of historical figures. Two writers who have studied Carnegie's career with the benefit of hindsight are the economist Robert Heilbroner and the historian Joseph Wall. While neither man is totally objective, each tries honestly, from his own perspective, to assess Carnegie's industrial achievement.

Robert Heilbroner was a professor of economics at the New School of Social Research in New York. While writing his book *The Quest for Wealth: A Study of Acquisitive Man* (published in 1956), he grew interested in Carnegie's career; and in an article for the popular history magazine *American Heritage* entitled "Epitaph for the Steel Master," he gave the following analysis of how Carnegie accomplished what he did.

> The actual process of growth involved every aspect of successful business enterprise of the times: acquisition and merger, pools and commercial piracy, and even, on one occasion, an outright fraud in selling the United States government overpriced and underdone steel armor plate. But it would be as foolish to maintain that the Carnegie empire grew by trickery as to deny that sharp practice had

its place. Essentially what lay behind the spectacular expansion were three facts.

The first of these was the sheer economic expansion of the industry in the first days of burgeoning steel use. Everywhere steel replaced iron or found new uses—and not only in railroads but in ships, buildings, bridges, machinery of all sorts. As Henry Frick himself once remarked, if the Carnegie group had not filled the need for steel another would have. But it must be admitted that Carnegie's company did its job superlatively well. In 1885 Great Britain led the world in the production of steel. Fourteen years later her total output was 695,000 tons less than the output of the Carnegie Steel Company alone.

Second was the brilliant assemblage of personal talent with which Carnegie surrounded himself. Among them, three in particular stood out. One was Captain William Jones, a Homeric figure who lumbered through the glowing fires and clanging machinery of the works like a kind of Paul Bunyan of steel, skilled at handling men, inventive in handling equipment, and enough of a natural artist to produce papers for the British Iron and Steel Institute that earned him a literary as well as a technical reputation. Then there was Henry Frick, himself a self-made millionaire, whose coke empire naturally complemented Carnegie's steelworks. When the two were amalgamated, Frick took over the active management of the whole, and under his forceful hand the annual output of the Carnegie works rose tenfold. Yet another was Charles Schwab, who came out of the tiny monastic town of Loretto, Pennsylvania, to take a job as a stake driver. Six months later he had been promoted by Jones into the assistant managership of the Braddock plant.

These men, and a score like them, constituted the vital energy of the Carnegie works. As Carnegie himself said, "Take away all our money, our great works, ore mines and coke ovens, but leave our organization, and in four years I shall have re-established myself."

But the third factor in the growth of the empire was Carnegie himself. A master salesman and a skilled diplomat of business at its highest levels, Carnegie was also a ruthless driver of his men. He pitted his associates and subordinates in competition with one another until a feverish atmosphere pervaded the whole organization. "You cannot imagine the abounding sense of freedom and relief I experience as soon as I get on board a steamer and sail past Sandy Hook," he once said to Captain Jones [referring to his trips to Europe]. "My God!" replied Jones. "Think of the relief to us!"

But Carnegie could win loyalties as well. All his promising young men were given gratis ownership participations—minuscule fractions of one per cent, which were enough, however, to make them millionaires in their own right. Deeply grateful to Jones, Carnegie once offered him a similar participation. Jones hemmed and hawed and finally refused; he would be unable to work effectively with the men, he said, once he was a partner. Carnegie insisted that his contribution be recognized and asked Jones what he wanted. "Well," said the latter, "you might pay me a hell of a big salary." "We'll do it!" said Carnegie. "From this time forth you shall receive the same salary as the President of the United States." "Ah, Andy, that's the kind of talk," said Captain Bill.

Within three decades, on the flood tide of economic expansion, propelled by brilliant work and relentless pressure from Carnegie, the company made immense strides. "Such a magnificent aggregation of industrial power has never before been under the domination of a single man," reported a biographer in 1902, describing the Gargantuan structure of steel and coke and ore and transport. Had the writer known of the profits earned by this aggregation he might have been even more impressed: three and a half million dollars in 1889, seven million in 1897, twenty-one million in 1899, and an immense forty million in 1900. "Where is there such a business!" Carnegie had exulted, and no wonder—the majority share of all these earnings, without hindrance of income tax, went directly into his pockets.

The historian Joseph Frazier Wall made the most thorough study so far of Andrew Carnegie and his industrial career. His biography *Andrew Carngeie,* published in 1970, ran to over 1,100 pages. In the following selection he considered whether robber baron or the later term "industrial statesman" more accurately described Carnegie. The latter was used by historians in the second half of the twentieth century when they credited the industrialists with creating the power for America to help win two world wars. Carnegie, Wall said, knew of the term robber baron and intensely disliked it. He believed that his industrial organization provided the public with great economic benefits. He would have agreed with the term industrial statesman had he lived long enough to hear it. If anyone were being robbed, Carnegie always believed, it was himself. He could have made far greater profits than he did. Wall also discussed the extravagant and wasteful ways of the American industrialists, ways that made them fabulously rich way their European counterparts found appalling.

> The arguments used by both Carnegie and the later revisionist historians against the use of the term "robber baron" are at best only partial truths and fail to get at the real error in the metaphor. If Carnegie was not robbing the consumer in selling steel at one cent a pound, he was certainly not being robbed. His annual profits would indicate

that his cost for producing steel, even with all the preliminary trans-
actions in obtaining the raw materials, as he outlined them, was considerably below one cent a pound. As he acquired the ownership of
sources of raw materials and transportation facilities, the difference
between cost of production and market price became ever greater, of
course, with the result that Carnegie's annual profits in a period of
five years increased by over 500 per cent.

As for the "industrial statesmanship" thesis of the revisionist historians, it comes perilously close to being based on the logical falla-
cy of *post hoc, ergo propter hoc* [a popular Latin epigram meaning
"after it happens, intention is assumed"]. Certainly Carnegie was not
thinking of his nation's needs fifty years hence as his steam shovels
clawed the very best surface ore out of the Mesabi Range at an ever-
increasing rate. Indeed, so rapidly did the amount of tonnage taken
out of the range increase that even Oliver [head of the company
that mined ore for the Carnegie mills] became alarmed at the rate at
which the Carnegie Steel mills were using up the best Bessemer
ores of Mesabi. He counseled, "It is not a wise policy to quickly
exhaust the rich quarry we have on the Mesaba Range, taking off
rapidly the surface ore." He urged Frick and Carnegie to "look to the
future" and "prolong the period of cheap steam shovel mining" by
taking on other ores for mixture.

———

There is also an implied assumption in the "industrial statesman"
thesis that only the means the Rockefellers, Carnegies, Goulds, and
Harrimans employed could America have achieved its industrial
supremacy. Such a supposition cannot be sustained when subjected
to a comparative historical study of modern economic development. No other nation that has engaged in industrialization, since
Great Britain first led the way, has done so with as little planning
and with such a great waste of natural resources, manpower, and
capital as did the United States in the post Civil War period. Only
the uniquely favorable conditions of vast physical resources, unre-
stricted immigration, and the political security provided by her geo-
graphical location gave the United States the freedom to industrialize
in the manner in which she did. Every European visitor to America
in the late nineteenth century was appalled by the waste and lack
of order in America's industrialism. The great English steelmaker, Sir
Lowthian Bell, who visited the United States in 1890, could hardly
believe what he saw at Pittsburgh and Johnstown—the "recklessly
rapid rate of driving" blast furnaces that brought "the interiors to a
wreck about every three years."

Workers were driven and burned out with the same reckless dis-
regard. Hamlin Garland found not one man over forty in the steel

mill at Homestead. Sir James Kitson, the president of the British Iron and Steel Institute, also visited the United States in 1890. While inspecting one of Carnegie's works, he met a former employee of his, who told Kitson, "I am quite a different man here from what I was in the old country; I don't know why it is so. . . . I can do more work; I feel that I have it in me; but I also feel and know that it won't last. I shall be done in ten years." Kitson's conclusion, after visiting many mills, was, "No, it won't last. The extreme physical effort put forth results in greater productivity, but it saps the vital energies and cuts short the career. This continual work at high pressure does not pay in the end. It won't last; and the re-mark applies with equal force to the employers as well as to the workers."

———

It would be wrong to suggest [however] that [Carnegie's] ambition for building an empire of business was totally negative or destructive of the best interests of the nation. There was a pride in this creative activity that ensured certain standards of behavior and a certain quality of product which a Gould or a Drew would never understand. Carnegie was quite sincere when he said that he had never knowingly turned out a rail or structural beam that he was not proud to see his name stamped upon: "We are not in for dollars," Carnegie wrote to Schwab in January 1900. "Fortunately, you and I and all our partners have plenty, or are getting plenty. We have pleasure in business, performing useful parts-this is our great reward."

Carnegie, to be sure, was overly sanctimonious when he wrote this. He was always "in for dollars," and the accumulation of wealth was a major motivation for his business activity, as all his partners knew full well. But it was an over-simplification to answer the question of "What makes Andy or John D. run" with a dollar sign, as many of the Populists, Muckrakers, and the later New Dealers did. In so doing, these critics of "the economic royalists" failed to understand how intense and sustained this drive for economic success was among these titans of the business world. If the accumulation of dollars had been the sole motivation for Carnegie, Frick, or Rockefeller, this purpose would have been amply satisfied long before their business activities were actually concluded. As Carnegie said, "You and I have plenty." Carnegie found "pleasure in business," quite apart from monetary gain. Wealth, beyond a certain point, cannot be an end in itself. It serves only as a yardstick.

The desire for power, however, is not so easily satiated as is the desire for wealth. It is not subject to the same law of diminishing returns as is the acquisition and consumption of material goods. It was imperial power that Carnegie, Frick, and Rockefeller sought-empires of steel, coke, and oil in which each would reign supreme. . . .

DONALD TRUMP ON THE METHODOLOGY
OF THE MOGUL

Those who condemned the robber barons longed to return to a world where the worker truly prospered by his or her labor, where the rising young entrepreneur could carve his or her own place in the world of business, where the few who might have had the skills and good luck to grow fabulously rich were controlled for the sake of economic justice. Perhaps this "utopia" never really existed, but it exercised a powerful influence on reformers. Between 1900 and 1920 Progressive statesmen made rhetorical if sometimes empty threats to "bust" the trusts that had built up. After a brief return to the worship of wealth in the Roaring Twenties, when Barton wrote his book about Jesus, the Great Depression rocked America's faith in and admiration for the moguls. Murray Kempton once remarked that with the crash of the stock market Americans turned for guidance not to the new rich but to old money in the form of the slightly shabby but comfortingly noble Franklin D. Roosevelt. Roosevelt's New Deal brought a mild form of socialism to American life, mild indeed when compared to that of Europe, and many people believed that economic as well as political equality was at hand.

Yet since World War II, in the rising prosperity of the Cold War era, as the largest generation in American history came of age, a new type of mogul has emerged. In addition to automobiles and their various subsidiary enterprises, and high-tech commodities such as television and computers, the building trade has since 1950 been one of the most lucrative areas of growth. In that field there may be more successful, richer entrepreneurs, but there is none more recognizable than developer Donald Trump. Trump has no rags-to-riches story to tell because he was born to comfort; but he is the most popular, at least the most watched, of the modern moguls of the American scene.

In his book *The Art of the Comeback,* Trump wrote of how he made it to the top of the financial ladder a second time after a decline following his first great success. At the end of his account, he summarized all he had said with "Trump's Top Ten Comeback Tips," a guide to becoming a successful mogul and perhaps an American icon.

1. PLAY GOLF
   It helped me relax and concentrate. It took my mind off my problems; I only thought about putting the ball in the hole. And, the irony is, I made lots of money on the golf course—making contacts and deals and coming up with ideas.

2. STAY FOCUSED
I am convinced that if I had maintained the same work ethic I
had during the 1970s and most of the 1980s, there would have been
no recession for me. I wasn't focused and really thought that life
and success just came hand in hand. I thought I was better than the
rest. When I began to relax and take it a little—or perhaps a lot—
easier things began to fall apart. [In the text of his book he admitted
that he needed "certain God-given talents" but that "working hard is
often the common denominator for success."]

3. BE PARANOID
I have noticed over the years that people who are guarded or, to
put it more coldly, slightly paranoid, end up being the most successful. Let some paranoia reign! You've got to realize that you have
something other people want. Don't let them take it away.

4. BE PASSIONATE
This is a key ingredient to success and to coming back. If you
don't have passion about who you are, about what you are trying to
be, about where you are going, you might as well close this book
right now and give up. Go get a job and relax, because you have no
chance of making it. Passion is the essence of life and certainly the
essence of success.

5. GO AGAINST THE TIDE
When I decided to keep 40 Wall Street as an office building, everyone in lower Manhattan was converting their buildings to residential
space—and with good reason. The apartment market is hot as a pis-
tol. I decided to head in the exact opposite direction, and now I am
signing up tenants at rents far higher than anything I expected.

6. GO WITH YOUR GUT
Some of the greatest investors I have ever known invest by
instinct, rather than research, study, or hard work. If you look back
over history, this is the way the greatest fortunes have been built.
People had ideas that they truly believed in.

7. WORK WITH PEOPLE YOU LIKE
If you go to the office and don't find the energy in the people
you are with, it is highly unlikely that you will be energized toward
success.

8. BE LUCKY
I hate to put this in the book because it can't be acquired.
People who inherit fortunes are lucky; I call them members of the
lucky sperm club. But you can help coax luck into your life by
working hard and being at the right place at the right time.

9. GET EVEN

During the bad times, I learned who was loyal and who wasn't. I believe in an eye for an eye. A couple of people who betrayed me need my help now, and I am screwing them against the wall! I am doing a number . . . and I'm having so much fun.

10. ALWAYS HAVE A PRENUPTIAL AGREEMENT

Anyone in a complicated business should be institutionalized if he or she gets married without one. I know firsthand that you can't come back if you're spending all of your time fighting for your financial life with a spouse.

Having made some of the most profitable real estate investments of modern times, having taken and discarded several beautiful wives, Trump was able in the year 2000 to keep legions of news commentators on his watch for months while he hinted that he might run for President of the United States. No other candidate with his record of marital failure and peculiar personal phobias (he does not shake hands for fear of germs) would have been taken seriously. The comprehensive coverage had to have been due to his vast wealth. After all, billionaire Ross Perot garnered 19% of the popular vote for President in 1992, despite his personal and professional quirks. Americans seem still to admire and take seriously a mogul who has amassed a fortune, regardless of the person's life style and idiosyncrasies. For better or worse, Donald Trump, like Andrew Carnegie, is an American icon.

QUESTIONS FOR CRITICAL EXAMINATION

1. What do Carnegie's comments about business success reveal about the man, both personally and professionally? What subjects did he like to discuss publicly, what subjects did he avoid, and how did he arrange and interpret the facts to show himself in the most positive light?

2. Analyze Carnegie's story of the three-legged stool. Did it explain the world of industry in his day? What were its fallacies? Explain why Carnegie thought this address was appropriate for a place where his company had experienced industrial strife.

3. To what extent was Carnegie a risk-taker, and to what extent was he a careful, even conservative investor? How would his philosophy of putting all one's eggs in the same basket and then watching that basket work in today's American economic system?

4. What image of Carnegie did the *Cosmopolitan* article convey? How did Gleed reconcile the acquisitive, industrialist Carnegie with the beloved, "saintly" philanthropist? On what issues did Gleed probably consider Carnegie wrong, and why did he merely allude to his disagreements without going into detail about them?

5. Outline Bruce Barton's argument that Jesus was the forerunner of the modern American businessman. How did Barton reflect the opinions of his day? What fallacies do you find in his logic? What changes in his text, if any, would have to be made in order to publish his book today? Would it sell? How would your fellow students, if they were told that the book was new, respond to his arguments?

6. What picture of the American industrial and social scene of 1887 did Edward Bellamy paint? What did he believe was wrong with that system, and how did he account for the fact that it continued, with all its faults, to function? How did he predict it would be altered to provide equality and justice?

7. How did the Populists describe the economic picture of the late nineteenth century? What did they mean when they said it was corrupting all of American society? Who was to blame? How could it be remedied? Which of their ideas survived the demise of their party and were incorporated into the two major parties?

8. What did Justice Brandeis believe was the key to economic reform and success? How did he believe it could be achieved? What qualities do you find in his thought and literary style that enabled him to become such a strong spokesman for Progressivism?

9. What conclusions about Carnegie's industrial career did you draw from the analyses of Heilbroner and Wall? In what ways does the passing of time help scholars better understand a person and an era?

10. What do Donald Trump's "tips" tell you about Trump himself, the reasons for his success, and the contemporary American business world? How is Trump like and unlike Carnegie in philosophy and approach? How do you think Carnegie would respond to Trump—particularly the thought expressed in his sixth tip?

Chapter Four

THE SHAME OF HOMESTEAD: ANDREW CARNEGIE AS AMERICAN DISGRACE

> "No pangs remain of any wound received in my business career save that of Homestead."
>
> ANDREW CARNEGIE
> *Autobiography*

Having come from a poor family of political radicals, Andrew Carnegie considered himself a friend of working men. He believed that since he was born into the working class and had only in adulthood become an executive he understood workers and treated them fairly. As earlier noted, he also believed that his workers loved him.

In 1886 he wrote two articles for the publication *Forum* in which he outlined his attitudes toward the men who worked for him. He said they should have the right to form unions. He advocated a sliding scale of pay in which workers would share a percentage of profits. He said that strikes, in the unfortunate event that they came, should never be broken by management, especially not by using "scab" labor. He finished with an oratorical flourish, offering an eleventh commandment: "Thou shalt not take thy neighbor's job."

That same year, in his book *Triumphant Democracy,* he compared the British and American socioeconomic systems. He argued, artiulately and with evidence of having given thought to the topic, but without

reference to the way men worked in his plants, that the American system would triumph because the Charter, long denied to the British, had
been granted to the American people. Americans enjoyed freedom and
opportunity the British still waited to see. Monarchy and aristocracy
were doomed, he predicted, and democracy would triumph. America
was the land of working men, the country where every person, regardless of his birth, could make it big. The book was praised by most of its
reviewers, and Carnegie was gratified to see that he was recognized as
a unique individual: a captain of industry whose goal was to help the
working class reach the American dream.

But it was largely fiction. While he was born poor and had worked
his way up the ladder of success more easily than would have been
possible in Britain, the claim that he still thought like a working man
was false. Even as a young man, while working for his patron Thomas
Scott at Penn Rail, he spied for management and reported the names of
a group of men plotting a strike for higher wages. Scott had the men
arrested, the strike was averted, and Carnegie was rewarded. After this
betrayal he was never again a member of the working class, either in
the kind of work he did or in his attitude toward labor.

Throughout most of his adult life he lived in New York as a financier, not in Pittsburgh as a mill manager. He spent his days in financial
centers like Manhattan and London, not in America's industrial heart-
land where his men worked. Furthermore, he longed most of all to be
an intellectual, to escape the concerns even of industrial management,
and to a great degree he was successful in doing so. He occupied a
world quite distinct from that of the men who worked in his mills,
while he assumed and cultivated the image of a man risen from the
ranks whose major concern was the welfare of his workers.

The truth was quite different. The way Carnegie treated "his men"
was uneven—and for the most part heartless. He richly rewarded his
partners, the men who conferred with him in his executive offices and
managed his mills for him; and he made some of them wealthy,
although he always kept the lion's share of profits for himself. Skilled
laborers, mostly of British and German ancestry, the only ones ever represented by unions, he paid well enough by the standards of the day,
although he did not mind working them to exhaustion and as often as
possible tried to deal with them outside union rules. These men, who
shared many of his cultural values, he felt he could "charm" into following his directives. Unskilled laborers, likely to be of Southern and
Eastern European descent, he treated with barely concealed contempt,
believing that they could easily be replaced or would continue to work

Carnegie Library of Pittsburgh. Drawing "At the Base of the Blast Furnace" / Joseph Stella.

Artist Joseph Stella's candid drawing of the way men labored in Carnegie's mills.

for him regardless of conditions. Despite his claims of *noblesse oblige,* he was not a friend of the working poor.

Carnegie's mills were among the worst places in America to work. He made sure that they were continually renovated and outfitted with the latest equipment, assuring that they operated at peak capacity; but he permitted his workers to labor under rules and conditions now considered barbaric. In a study published in 1914 in Paul Underwood Kellogg's book *Wage Earning Pittsburgh,* H. F. J. Porter admitted that Carnegie was the best businessman in nineteenth-century steel production. He put competitors out of business through his foresight and administrative skills. Yet Porter noted that it was done at a "fearful human cost." Carnegie refused when he could avoid it to let his workers bargain collectively for better wages and working conditions, and he used spies to keep workers from organizing. Furthermore, work schedules at Carnegie Steel were inhumane. For example, the "long turn" plan, probably conceived by Carnegie's partner and plant CEO Henry Clay Frick, had men work twelve-hour days for twelve days running, a twenty-four hour thirteenth day, followed by twenty-four hours off. If during the last fortnight a worker had been on the day shift, the next he would be on the night shift and vice versa. This system was retained through the Carnegie years and into the 1920s under the successor United States Steel Corporation. Only in the Warren Harding administration, with pressure from the Federal Council of Churches, was it moderated.

The event known to history as "Homestead" should not have surprised Carnegie, his admirers, and much of the American and British public. It did so only because so many people, including Carnegie himself, believed the myth of benevolent management he had so carefully established and cultivated for himself.

THE STORY OF HOMESTEAD

The events of July 1892, at the Carnegie Steel Mills in Homestead, Pennsylvania, hit Carnegie hard. Although he went on making large piles of steel and money for another nine years, with even greater fervor than previously, as if to prove his worth to himself and the public, as if to shake free of the stigma of Homestead, he was never quite the same person in its aftermath. Although he denied personal responsibility for the violence of those summer days, he never shed his feelings of guilt for the suffering on both sides of the conflict. He sought from that time on to redeem his image through ever more numerous philanthropic endeavors. Homestead gave his admirers pause and his critics ammunition with which to attack his labor policies and accumulation of wealth at the expense of working men. It was, and still remains, the darkest cloud over Carnegie's industrial triumph. It tarnished his image as a benevolent manager of money and men, and it never completely went away.

Homestead fell into a category with two other industrial strikes of the same period, both of which were treated with equally sordid managerial response. In 1886 workers struck the McCormick Harvester Company, and a rally in support of the strikers at Chicago's Haymarket Square turned violent when a bomb was detonated. Government forces stepped in, ended the strike, and picked eight "anarchists" to take blame for the incident. In 1894 workers struck the Pullman Palace Car Company and held their own until President Grover Cleveland ordered federal troops to crush the rebellion. Homestead, coming between these two events, was identified with them, both by people sympathetic and unsympathetic to organized labor.

Carnegie held controlling financial interest in the Homestead plant; but during the summer of 1892 he was on his usual extended holiday at his castle in Scotland, and his partner Henry Clay Frick was in complete charge of operations. The Amalgamated Iron and Steel Workers Union represented the skilled laborers at Homestead, and in the past Carnegie had himself agreed, despite his usual reluctance, to contracts with the union. The latest of the contracts was to end July 1, 1892. Frick, who hated unions—Carnegie merely found them an annoyance—was determined to break this one. He had only to get Carnegie's permission to use force.

As he left for his Scottish vacation in June, Carnegie apparently agreed with Frick that when the Homestead contract ended on July 1, Homestead should be reorganized with nonunion labor. He left it completely in Frick's hands how this was to be accomplished. On his own, but sure of Carnegie's blessings, Frick decided not to negotiate with Amalgamated, to close the plant on July 1, and to reopen it July 7 as a nonunion shop. He fortified the plant's walls and hired the Pinkerton Detective Agency to bring in three hundred armed troops by river barges on July 6 to keep order when the new terms were announced. Former employees who accepted the new terms would be rehired, those who did not would be terminated. He expected all of the unskilled workers, who were nonunion anyway, to accept his terms in order to keep their jobs. He expected to lose many of the skilled workers, but without them he would be able to eliminate all union influence and train new men.

In several ways he was wrong. Word leaked about his upcoming plan. Skilled and unskilled workers remained united, occupied land around the plant, and by the time the Pinkertons arrived at 4 a.m. on July 6 had retaken the plant itself. As soon as the barges landed, workers fired on them from the protection of furnaces and piles of iron. The shooting went on all day, until the Pinkertons agreed to surrender their arms in exchange for safe passage out of town. They were forced to run a gauntlet of workers with clubs and after their beating were locked in the town's Opera House while the nearest sheriff was summoned. Three Pinkertons and ten workers died that day, thirty more Pinkertons were seriously wounded, and none left Homestead without some injury. The number of workers injured was never accurately counted or reported, but it was believed by all sides to be high.

A *New York Times* account of the day's events was chilling. Titled "Mob Law at Homestead," it was far more concerned with the fate of the Pinkertons on their barges than with that of the workers at the mill, yet it admitted that the violence was initiated by Frick's decision to bring in Pinkertons to carry out his plan to break the union. Through the morning, the writer said, the workers fired rifles and even cannons at the boats. Then they changed tactics.

> When it was found that little impression could be made by the cannon on the boats an effort was made to fire the barges and thus compel the detectives to leave the vessel or suffer the terrible fate of being burned alive. Hose was procured and oil was spouted on the docks and sides of the barges.
>
> While this was done barrel after barrel of oil was emptied into the river above the mooring place, the object being to allow it to float against the boats and then ignite it. This was attempted several times, but the boats did not burn, and then the mob hurled dynamite bombs at them.
>
> Finally it was evident to everybody that they would soon die if they were not relieved, and the leadership of the strikers pleaded with their followers to allow the Pinkertons to surrender.
>
> The appeal was drowned with shouts of "No!" "No!" "We'll kill them like dogs!" "They shall have no mercy!" but when, a few minutes later, the white handkerchief appeared on the top of one of the barges, the firing ceased and the strikers consented to a parley.
>
> The Pinkerton men, as soon as they found it was safe to talk, offered to surrender if the leaders guaranteed them protection. The promise was given, and 266 men marched off the boat and gave up their arms.
>
> The promise that they should not be harmed seemed to be forgotten. They were driven like sheep between lines of strikers to the Opera House. All the way they were beaten first with fists, and then with clubs, and every conceivable weapon. Every man was sore and covered with blood before he found shelter.

It sounds from this account as though the workers won, but the opposite proved true. On July 12, the governor brought in the Pennsylvania National Guard, eight thousand strong, restoring Frick's authority. On July 15, the plant reopened as a nonunion shop. Only two in five former employees were rehired, and Amalgamated gave up claim to represent anyone at Homestead. In the remaining nine years of Carnegie's career, not a single worker in any of his mills was represented by a union, and not until the New Deal of the 1930s were unions permitted inside the mills of United States Steel.

When Carnegie received word of the violence on July 6, he wired Frick that he would return immediately to mediate the issue; but Frick urged him to stay in Scotland. Carnegie's feelings and actions were ambivalent. Recounted in Livesay's *Andrew Carnegie: The Rise of Business* (p. 142). He wired to Frick unequivocal approval of his action at Homestead: "All anxiety gone since you stand firm. Never employ one of these rioters. Let grass grow over works. . . . " Publicly he also expressed support for Frick, and many years passed before he said anything differently. Yet privately, even at the time, he told intimates that Frick had taken a "foolish step" and that he did not approve of it. He said to his closest associates, "The pain I suffer increases daily. The works are not worth one drop of human blood. I wish they had sunk." He knew his name was tarnished by Homestead, and he began immediately to try to restore it.

On his return to the United States at the end of the summer, Carnegie went directly to Pittsburgh and made a tour of his mills, including Homestead. The workers received him graciously, but they reviled Frick. One man said to him, "Oh Mr. Carnegie, it wasn't a question of dollars. The boys would have let you kick 'em, but they wouldn't let that other man stroke their hair." The *New York Times* reporter on the scene indicated that even at the height of the gun battle Carnegie's workers believed that had he been there instead of Frick the trouble would have been avoided. While the *Times* writer editorialized that Carnegie was at fault for going off to Scotland when trouble was brewing, the men at the plant did not seem to blame him.

Carnegie was perhaps the last of the old bosses, one who had risen from labor himself, one the men trusted, even when he betrayed them. But the future lay with the Fricks, who made not even a pretense of caring for the masses. Carnegie never again trusted Frick, and the two eventually parted ways with acrimonious lawsuits. For his part, after Homestead Carnegie seemed to double his efforts both in production and in paternalism. He steered his mills through the depression era of 1893–1897 and added to his personal fortune. He began granting money for libraries and schools to communities where his workers lived, and he offered the men mistreated at Homestead pensions. His philanthropy was certainly an attempt to put Homestead to rest. Yet he never was able to shake the event. "I was the controlling owner," he said much later. "That was sufficient to make my name a by-word for years."

THE "TRIAL" OF CARNEGIE'S LIFE

In the *Autobiography* he wrote in his later years, Carnegie devoted a chapter to "The Problems of Labor." There, as if trying to show that had he been at Homestead the trouble would have been averted, he described the way he handled working men, how his charm always carried the day. In one case, as the threat of a strike loomed, he met with a committee of thirty-two workers to discuss the new wage offer he had made.

> The Committee came from the works to meet me at the office in Pittsburgh. The proceedings were opened by one of our best men, Billy Edwards (I remember him well; he rose to high position afterwards), who thought that the total offered was fair, but that the scale was not equable. Some departments were all right, others were not fairly dealt with. Most of the men were naturally of this opinion, but when they came to indicate the underpaid, there was a difference, as was to be expected. No two men in the different departments could agree. Billy began:
>
> "Mr. Carnegie, we agree that the total sum per ton to be paid is fair, but we think it is not properly distributed among us. Now, Mr. Carnegie, you take my job—"
>
> "Order, order!" I cried. "None of that, Billy. Mr. Carnegie 'takes no man's job.' Taking another's job is an unpardonable offense among high-classed workmen."
>
> There was loud laughter, followed by applause, and then more laughter. I laughed with them. We had scored on Billy. Of course the dispute was soon settled. It is not solely, often it is not chiefly, a matter of dollars with workmen. Appreciation, kind treatment, a fair deal—these are often the potent forces with the American workmen.

Carnegie's contention in the *Forum* articles that he did not believe in breaking strikes was patently false. He broke every one he could. He said that he despised unions because they represented only part of the work force, the hardest to control, those least likely to accept his explanations about profits and wages, and that as a beloved employer (benevolent dictator might be a better term) he could go to the workers and convince them to accept his terms. The following story about another labor dispute tells it all.

> The way a strike was once broken at our steel-rail mills is interesting. Here again, I am sorry to say, one hundred and thirty-four men in one department had bound themselves under secret oath to demand increased wages at the end of the year, several months away. The new year proved very unfavorable for business, and other iron and steel manufacturers throughout the country had effected reductions in wages. Nevertheless, these men, having secretly sworn months previously that they would not work unless they got increased wages, thought themselves bound to insist upon their demands. We could not advance wages when our competitors were reducing them, and the works were stopped in consequence. Every department of the works was brought to a stand by these strikers.

The blast furnaces were abandoned a day or two before the time agreed upon, and we were greatly troubled in consequence.

I went to Pittsburgh and was surprised to find the furnaces had been banked, contrary to agreement. I was to meet the men in the morning upon arrival at Pittsburgh, but a message was sent to me from the works stating that the men had "left the furnaces and would meet me tomorrow." Here was a nice reception! My reply was:

"No, they won't. Tell them I shall not be here to-morrow. Anybody can stop work; the trick is to start it again. Some fine day these men will want the works started, and will be looking around for somebody who can start them, and I will tell them then just what I do now: that the works will never start except upon a sliding scale based upon the prices we get for our products. That scale will last three years and it will not be submitted by the men. They have submitted many scales to us. It is our turn now, and we are going to submit a scale to them.

"Now," I said to my partners, "I am going back to New York in the afternoon. Nothing more is to be done."

A short time after my message was received by the men they asked if they could come in and see me that afternoon before I left.

I answered: "Certainly!"

They came in and I said to them:

"Gentlemen, your chairman here, Mr. Bennett, assured you that I would make my appearance and settle with you in some way or other, as I always have settled. That is true. And he told you that I would not fight, which is also true. He is a true prophet. But he told you something else in which he was slightly mistaken. He said I *could* not fight. Gentlemen," looking Mr. Bennett straight in the eye and closing and raising my fist, "he forgot that I was Scotch. But I will tell you something; I will never fight you. I know better than to fight labor. I will not fight, but I can beat any committee that was ever made at sitting down, and I have sat down. These works will never start until the men vote by a two-thirds majority to start them, and then, as I told you this morning, they will start on our sliding scale. I have nothing more to say."

They retired. It was about two weeks afterwards that one of the house servants came to my library in New York with a card, and I found upon it the names of two of our workmen, and also the name of a reverend gentleman. The men said they were from the works at Pittsburgh and would like to see me.

"Ask if either of these gentlemen belongs to the blast-furnace workers who banked the furnaces contrary to agreement."

The man returned and said "No." I replied: "In that case go down and tell them that I shall be pleased to have them come up."

Of course they were received with genuine warmth and cordiality and we sat and talked about New York, for some time, this being their first visit.

"Mr. Carnegie, we really came to talk about the trouble at the works," the minister said at last.

"Oh, indeed!" I answered. "Have the men voted?"

"No," he said.

My rejoinder was:

"You will have to excuse me from entering upon that subject; I said I would never discuss it until they voted by a two-thirds majority to start the mills. Gentlemen, you have never seen New York. Let me take you out and show you Fifth Avenue and the Park, and we shall come back here to lunch at half-past one."

This we did, talking about everything except the one thing that they wished to talk about. We had a good time, and I know they enjoyed their lunch. There is one great difference between the American working-man and the foreigner. The American is a man; he sits down at lunch with people as if he were (as he generally is) a gentleman born. It is splendid.

They returned to Pittsburgh, not another word having been said about the works. But the men soon voted (there were very few votes against starting) and I went again to Pittsburgh. I laid before the committee the scale under which they were to work. It was a sliding scale based on the price of the product. Such a scale really makes capital and labor partners, sharing prosperous and disastrous times together. Of course it has a minimum, so that the men are always sure of living wages. As the men had seen these scales, it was unnecessary to go over them. The chairman said:

"Mr. Carnegie, we will agree to everything. And now," he said hesitatingly, "we have one favor to ask of you, and we hope you will not refuse it."

"Well, gentlemen, if it be reasonable I shall surely grant it."

"Well, it is this: That you permit the officers of the union to sign these papers for the men."

"Why, certainly, gentlemen! With the greatest pleasure! And then I have a small favor to ask of you, which I hope you will not refuse, as I have granted yours. Just to please me, after the officers have signed, let every workman sign also for himself. You see, Mr. Bennett, this scale lasts for three years, and some man, or body of men, might dispute whether your president of the union had authority to bind them for so long, but if we have his signature also, there cannot be any misunderstanding."

There was a pause; then one man at his side whispered to Mr. Bennett (but I heard him perfectly):

"By golly, the jig's up!"

So it was, but it was not by direct attack, but by a flank movement. Had I not allowed the union officers to sign, they would have
had a grievance and an excuse for war. As it was, having allowed
them to do so, how could they refuse so simple a request as mine,
that each free and independent American citizen should also sign
for himself. My recollection is that as a matter of fact the officers of
the union never signed, but they may have done so. Why should
they, if every man's signature was required? Besides this, the workmen, knowing that the union could do nothing for them when the
scale was adopted, neglected to pay dues and the union was desert-
ed. We never heard of it again. . . .

Carnegie was certain that as a benevolent employer he always did
his best for his workers, even when they did not recognize the wisdom
of his actions, and he resented union attempts to bargain for them.
Perhaps this explains why he was willing to let Frick deal so harshly
with the Homestead crisis, coming as it did when a union was trying to
negotiate a new contract at one of his plants. Whatever his motives for
permitting the fiasco at Homestead, he never stopped trying to explain
his actions there. At the time he called it " the trial of my life," and when
in old age he wrote his *Autobiography* he devoted another chapter
entirely to it. The following is his final attempt at self-defense for his
most indefensible public performance.

While upon the subject of our manufacturing interests, I may record
that on July 1, 1892, during my absence in the Highlands of
Scotland, there occurred the one really serious quarrel with our
workmen in our whole history. For twenty-six years I had been
actively in charge of the relations between ourselves and our men,
and it was the pride of my life to think how delightfully satisfactory
these had been and were. I hope I fully deserved what my chief
partner, Mr. Phipps, said in his letter to the "New York Herald,"
January 30, 1904, in reply to one who had declared I had remained
abroad during the Homestead strike, instead of flying back to support my partners. It was to the effect that "I was always disposed to
yield to the demands of the men, however unreasonable"; hence
one or two of my partners did not wish me to return. Taking no
account of the reward that comes from feeling that you and your
employees are friends and judging only from economical results, I
believe that higher wages to men who respect their employers and
are happy and contented are a good investment, yielding, indeed, big
dividends.

Carnegie then explained the situation at Homestead as he saw it.
During the three years of the old contract the mill had invested in new,

more efficient machinery, which could produce 60% more steel tonnage and thus that much more profits than earlier. Skilled laborers, paid
by the tonnage, were offered a 30% raise with another 30% going to pay
for the investment in new machinery. The union demanded the full
60% go to the skilled workers. Carnegie considered this unfair, even an
"attempt to extort."

> Up to this point all had been right enough. The policy I had pur-
> sued in cases of difference with our men was that of patiently wait-
> ing, reasoning with them, and showing them that their demands
> were unfair; but never attempting to employ new men in their
> places—never. The superintendent of Homestead, however, was
> assured by the three thousand men who were not concerned in the
> dispute that they would run the works, and were anxious to rid
> themselves of the two hundred and eighteen men who had banded
> themselves into a union and into which they had hitherto refused to
> admit those in other departments—only the "heaters" and "rollers"
> of steel being eligible.
>
> My partners were misled by this superintendent, who was him-
> self misled. He had not had great experience in such affairs, having
> recently been promoted from a subordinate position. The unjust
> demands of the few union men, and the opinion of the three thou-
> sand non-union men that they were unjust, very naturally led him
> into thinking there would be no trouble and that the workmen
> would do as they had promised. There were many men among the
> three thousand who could take, and wished to take, the places of
> the two hundred and eighteen—at least so it was reported to me.
>
> It is easy to look back and say that the vital step of opening the
> works should never have been taken. All the firm had to do was to
> say to the men: "There is a labor dispute here and you must settle it
> between yourselves. The firm has made you a most liberal offer. The
> works will run when the dispute is adjusted, and not till then.
> Meanwhile your places remain open to you." Or it might have been
> well if the superintendent had said to the three thousand men, "All
> right, if you will come and run the works without protection," thus
> throwing upon them the responsibility of protecting themselves—
> three thousand men as against two hundred and eighteen. Instead
> of this it was thought advisable (as an additional precaution by the
> state officials, I understand) to have the sheriff with guards to pro-
> tect the thousands against the hundreds. The leaders of the latter
> were violent and aggressive men; they had guns and pistols, and, as
> was soon proved, were able to intimidate the thousands.
>
> I quote what I once laid down in writing as our rule: "My idea is
> that the Company should be known as determined to let the men at
> any works stop work; that it will confer freely with them and wait

patiently until they decide to return to work, never thinking of trying new men—never." The best men as men, and the best workmen, are not walking the streets looking for work. Only the inferior class as a rule is idle. The kind of men we desired are rarely allowed to lose their jobs, even in dull times. It is impossible to get new men to run successfully the complicated machinery of a modern steel plant. The attempt to put in new men converted the thousands of old men who desired to work, into lukewarm supporters of our policy, for workmen can always be relied upon to resent the employment of new men. Who can blame them?

If I had been at home, however, I might have been persuaded to open the works, as the superintendent desired, to test whether our old men would go to work as they had promised. But it should be noted that the works were not opened at first by my partners for new men. On the contrary, it was, as I was informed upon my return, at the wish of the thousands of our old men that they were opened. This is a vital point. My partners were in no way blamable for making the trial so recommended by the superintendent. Our rule never to employ new men, but to wait for the old to return, had not been violated so far. In regard to the second opening of the works, after the strikers had shot the sheriff's officers, it is also easy to look back and say, "How much better had the works been closed until the old men voted to return"; but the Governor of Pennsylvania, with eight thousand troops, had meanwhile taken charge of the situation.

I was traveling in the Highlands of Scotland when the trouble arose, and did not hear of it until two days after. Nothing I have ever had to meet in all my life, before or since, wounded me so deeply. No pangs remain of any wound received in my business career save that of Homestead. It was so unnecessary. The men were outrageously wrong. The strikers, with the new machinery, would have made from four to nine dollars a day under the new scale—thirty per cent more than they were making with the old machinery. While in Scotland I received the following cable from the officers of the union of our workmen:

"Kind master, tell us what you wish us to do and we shall do it for you."

This was most touching, but, alas, too late. The mischief was done, the works were in the hands of the Governor; it was too late.

———

The general public, of course, did not know that I was in Scotland and knew nothing of the initial trouble at Homestead. Workmen had been killed at the Carnegie Works, of which I was the controlling owner. That was sufficient to make my name a by-word for years. . . .

———

A mass meeting of the workmen and their wives was afterwards
held in the Library Hall at Pittsburgh to greet me, and I addressed
them from both my head and my heart. The one sentence I remember, and always shall, was to the effect that capital, labor, and
employer were a three-legged stool, none before or after the others,
all equally indispensable. Then came the cordial hand-shaking and
all was well. Having thus rejoined hands and hearts with our
employees and their wives, I felt that a great weight had been effec-
tually lifted, but I had had a terrible experience although thousands
of miles from the scene.

Carnegie tried to dismiss Homestead as an aberration, an unfortunate event that he could have averted had he been on the scene. He
was not to blame for leaving the mill at a moment of inevitable crisis.
Despite Homestead, he was the friend of the working man. So he
hoped history would say.

CARNEGIE'S HOMESTEAD SHAME
IN THE AMERICAN POPULAR IMAGINATION

Conservative, mostly Republican, admirers of the captains of industry
were hard put to explain Homestead. When they did speak of it, they
found fault with the union for representing only skilled workers while
they condemned the unskilled workers of Slavic and Italian descent as
violent barbarians. They said the "owners" of mills had the right to
decide wages and defend their property against renegades and that
Homestead was proof of the dangers of unionism. Democrats used the
negative fallout from Homestead in their successful campaign to unseat
incumbent Republican President Benjamin Harrison in the 1892 election; and Republicans who lost Congressional seats that fall whispered
bitterly that the "arch-sneak" Carnegie had given their opponents
ammunition against them.

COMMENTARY IN THE *ST. LOUIS POST-DISPATCH*

Few people, even conservatives, excused Carnegie's absence or credited his claims of innocence. He was castigated both in Britain and the
United States for his absence during the crisis. A particularly scathing
review of the incident appeared in the *St. Louis Post-Dispatch* the following September. It is interesting that the writer, obviously sympathetic to the Homestead workers, expressed grudging admiration for

Henry Clay Frick while condemning Carnegie, the man he believed
gave the orders and then tried to hide from the consequences.

> Count no man happy until he is dead. Three months ago Andrew
> Carnegie was a man to be envied. Today he is an object of mingled
> pity and contempt. In the estimation of nine-tenths of the thinking
> people on both sides of the ocean he had not only given the lie to
> all his antecedents, but confessed himself a moral coward. One
> would naturally suppose that if he had a grain of consistency, not to
> say decency, in his composition, he would favor rather than oppose
> the organization of trades-unions among his own working people at
> Homestead. One would naturally suppose that if he had a grain of
> manhood, not to say courage, in his composition, he would at least
> have been willing to face the consequences of his inconsistency.
> But what does Carnegie do? Runs off to Scotland out of harm's way
> to await the issue of the battle he was too pusillanimous to share. A
> single word from him might have saved the bloodshed—but the
> word was never spoken. Nor has he, from that bloody day until this,
> said anything except that he had "implicit confidence in the man-
> agers of the mills." The correspondent who finally obtained this
> valuable information expresses the opinion that "Mr. Carnegie has
> no intention of returning to America at present." He might have
> added that America can well spare Mr. Carnegie. Ten thousand
> "Carnegie Public Libraries" would not compensate the country for
> the direct and indirect evils resulting from the Homestead lockout.
> Say what you will of Frick, he is a brave man. Say what you will of
> Carnegie, he is a coward. And gods and men hate cowards.

ANARCHIST EMMA GOLDMAN'S RESPONSE

Homestead shocked and spurred to action the most radical political
groups in America, chief among them the Anarchists. Most of them foreign born, Anarchists considered all political and economic powers
harmful to man. Living in Massachusetts at that time were Emma
Goldman and her lover Alexander Berkman, whom Emma called Sasha.
Emma was working in an ice cream shop, saving money for passage
back to her native Russia, hoping to help precipitate a revolution
against the tsar. Then came Homestead. In the following selection from
her autobiography *Living My Life,* published in 1913, Goldman
described the reaction of her comrades to the story coming from
Pennsylvania.

> It was May 1892. News from Pittsburgh announced that trouble had
> broken out between the Carnegie Steel Company and its employees
> organized in the Amalgamated Association of Iron and Steel Workers.

It was one of the biggest and most efficient labour bodies of the country, consisting mostly of Americans, men of decision and grit, who would assert their rights. The Carnegie Company, on the other hand, was a powerful corporation, known as a hard master. It was particularly significant that Andrew Carnegie, its president, had temporarily turned over the entire management to the company's chairman, Henry Clay Frick, a man known for his enmity to labour. Frick was also the owner of extensive coke-fields, where unions were prohibited and the workers were ruled with an iron hand.

———

The philanthropic Andrew Carnegie conveniently retired to his castle in Scotland, and Frick took full charge of the situation. He declared that henceforth the sliding scale would be abolished. The company would make no more agreements with the Amalgamated Association; it would itself determine the wages to be paid. In fact, he would not recognize the union at all. He would not treat with the employees collectively, as before. He would close the mills, and the men might consider themselves discharged. Thereafter they would have to apply for work individually, and the pay would be arranged with every worker separately. Frick curtly refused the peace advances of the workers' organization, declaring that there was "nothing to arbitrate." Not a strike, but a lockout," Frick announced. It was an open declaration of war.

Feeling ran high in Homestead and vicinity. The sympathy of the entire country was with the men. Even the most conservative part of the press condemned Frick for his arbitrary and drastic methods. They charged him with deliberately provoking a crisis that might assume national proportions, in view of the great numbers of men locked out by Frick's action, and the probable effect upon affiliated unions and on related industries.

Labour throughout the country was aroused. The steel-workers declared that they were ready to take up the challenge of Frick: they would insist on their right to organize and to deal collectively with their employers. Their tone was manly, ringing with the spirit of their rebellious forebears of the Revolutionary War.

Far away from the scene of the impending struggle, in our little ice-cream parlour in the city of Worcester, we eagerly followed developments. To us it sounded the awakening of the American worker, the long-awaited day of his resurrection. The native toiler had risen, he was beginning to feel his mighty strength, he was determined to break the chains that had held him in bondage so long, we thought. Our hearts were fired with admiration for the men of Homestead.

———

One afternoon a customer came in for an ice-cream, while I was alone in the store. As I set the dish down before him, I caught the large headlines of his paper: "LATEST DEVELOPMENTS IN HOME-STEAD—FAMILIES OF STRIKERS EVICTED FROM THE COMPANY HOUSES—WOMAN IN CONFINEMENT CARRIED OUT INTO THE STREET BY SHEFIFFS." I read over the man's shoulder Frick's dictum to the workers: he would rather see them dead than concede to their demands, and he threatened to import Pinkerton detectives. The brutal bluntness of the account, the inhumanity of Frick towards the evicted mother, inflamed my mind. Indignation swept my whole being. . . .

———

I locked up the store and ran full speed the three blocks to our little flat. It was Homestead, not Russia; I knew it now. We belonged in Homestead. The boys, resting for the evening shift, sat up as I rushed into the room, newspaper clutched in my hand. "What has happened, Emma? You look terrible!" I could not speak. I handed them the paper.

Sasha was the first on his feet. "Homestead!" he exclaimed. "I must go to Homestead!" I flung my arms around him, crying out his name. I, too, would go. "We must go tonight," he said; "the great moment has come at last!: Being internationalists, he added, it mattered not to us where the blow was struck by the workers; we must be with them. We must bring them our great message and help them see that it was not only for the moment that they must strike, but for all time, for a free life, for anarchism. Russia had many heroic men and women, but who was there in America? Yes, we must go to Homestead, tonight!

As it turned out, Emma did not go to Pittsburgh, but Berkman did. He was able within days after the Homestead event to get into the Carnegie offices and fire three bullets into Frick. Frick did not die. His image may actually have been slightly improved by the fact that an Anarchist tried to kill him, making him appear to be a symbol of order in a chaotic world. Berkman was sentenced to twenty-two years in prison. Because of her association with him and because she continued to make speeches calling for the violent overthrow of the American economic regime, Goldman herself spent a year in prison and was eventually deported. The United States was not big enough for both Carnegie Steel and Emma Goldman.

SOCIALIST EUGENE V. DEBS'S INDICTMENT

A further condemnation of Homestead came from labor spokesman Eugene V. Debs. Debs started work at age 16 as a railroad fireman and soon became a local union officer, on his way toward helping found the

Industrial Workers of the World union and later the Socialist Party. He ran for President of the United States five times. When Debs publicly defended labor leaders accused of using violent means to achieve economic advantages, President Theodore Roosevelt called him an "inciter to murder." When he publicly opposed U.S. involvement in World War I, President Woodrow Wilson called Debs a "traitor to his country," and he was imprisoned for sedition. Debs was editor of the *Locomotive Firemen's Magazine* in 1892 when he wrote the following article in response to the events at Homestead.

> The 4,000 employees of Carnegie & Com., at Homestead, Pennsylvania, have been engaged for years in pouring capital into the lap of capital, content if they could build for themselves humble homes, obtain the necessities of life, rear their children as becomes American citizens, and save a few dollars for a rainy day, for sickness and old age, and secure for themselves a decent burial.
>
> By virtue of their brain and brawn, their skill and muscle, their fidelity to duty, Homestead grew in importance. It obtained a world-wide fame. The chief proprietor, Andrew Carnegie, a Scotchman by birth, an aristocrat by inclination, and a Christian with Christ omitted, waxed fat in wealth while the men toiled on. The works spread out, area expanded, buildings and machinery increased, night and day the forges blazed and roared, the anvils rang, wheels revolved, and still Carnegie grew in opulence. Taking his place among the millionaires of the world, he visits his native land and sensation follows sensation as he dazzles lords and ladies, dukes and dudes by the display of his wealth in highland and lowland.

> Andrew Carnegie, who for a quarter of a century has coined the sweat and blood and the life of thousands into wealth until his fortune exceeds many times a million, proclaims "that upon the sacredness of property civilization itself depends." This Carnegie, a combination of flint and steel, plutocrat and pirate, Scotch terrier and English bulldog, rioting in religious rascality, attempts to show that he is animated by "Christ's spirit," and remembering that when Christ wanted "tribute money" to satisfy Caesar, He told Peter to go to the sea and cast a hook, catch a fish and in its mouth the required funds would be found, Carnegie and his Phipps and Frick, wanting cash wherewith to pay tribute to Mammon, have cast hooks into the sea of labor and securing from 5,000 to 10,000 bites a day, have hauled in that number of workingmen and taken from their mouths such sums as their greed demanded wherewith to enlarge their fortunes and enable them with autocratic pomp and parade, to take the place of Jumbos in the procession.

———

The day of the lockout came, July 1, 1892. The steel works at Homestead were silent as a cemetery. The workingmen were remanded to idleness. Their offense was that they wanted fair wages—the old scale—and that they were members of a powerful labor organization, created to resist degradation.

Between July 1 and the morning of July 6, unrest was universal; excitement increased with every pulsebeat. The workingmen had charge of Homestead. Frick was in exile, but he was not quiet. He wanted possession of the steel works. His purpose was to introduce scabs, to man Fort Frick; to get his dynamos to work and send streams of electricity along the barbed wires, to touch which was death. He wanted to have seas of hot water to be sent on its scalding, death-dealing mission if a discharged workingman approached the works. He wanted the muzzle of a Winchester rifle at every porthold in the fence, and behind it a thug to send a quieting bullet through the head or the heart of any man who deemed it prudent to resist oppression.

What was the scheme? To introduce Pinkerton thugs armed with Winchester rifles, a motley gang of vagabonds mustered from the slums of the great cities: pimps and parasites, outcasts, abandoned wretches of every grade; a class of characterless cutthroats who murder for hire; creatures in the form of humans but as heartless as stones. Frick's reliance was upon an army of Christless whelps to carry into effect Carnegie's "Gospel of Wealth."

Oh, men who wear the badge of labor! Now is the time for you in fancy at least to go to Homestead. You need to take in the picture of this little town on the bank of the Monongahela. You peer through the morning mists and behold the Frick flotilla approaching, bearing to the landing 300 armed Pinkertons, each thug with a Winchester and all necessary ammunition to murder Homestead workingmen. The plot of Frick was hellish from its inception. There is nothing to parallel it in conflicts labor has had since Noah built his ark. No man with a heart in him can contemplate Frick's scheme without a shudder.

The alarm had been sounded. The Homestead workingmen were on the alert. They were the "minute men" such as resisted the British troops at Concord and Lexington in 1775. The crisis had come. Nearer and nearer approached Frick's thugs. Four thousand workingmen are on guard. Now, for Carnegie's "Gospel of Wealth." In quick succession rifle reports ring out from the "Model Barges" and workingmen bite the dust. Homestead is now something more than the seat of the Carnegie steel works. It is a battlefield, and from Thermopylae to Waterloo, from Concord to Yorktown, from Bull's Run to Appomattox there is not one which to workingmen is so fraught with serious significance.

Amidst fire and smoke, blood and dying groans, the workingmen
stood their ground with Spartan courage. It was shot for shot, and
the battle continued until Frick's thugs surrendered and left the
workingmen at Homestead masters of the field. A number of the
thugs were killed, others were wounded and the remainder, demoralized, were glad to surrender and return to the slums from which
they were hired by Frick.

Rid of the gang of mercenary murderers, the workingmen proceeded to bury their dead comrades, the gallant men who preferred
death to degradation, and who are as deserving of monuments as
was ever a soldier who died in defense of country, flag or home. Of
these, there were ten who were killed outright on the morning of
the battle.

The fiend Frick, of coke region infamy, is the man directly responsible for the Homestead tragedies, and the blood of the murdered
men are blotches upon his soul, which the fires of hell will only make
more distinct, and still this monster simply represents a class of
Christless capitalists who are now engaged in degrading workingmen
for the purpose of filching from them a portion of their earnings that
they may roll in luxuries which wealth purchases.

Carnegie wires from his triumphal march through Scotland that
he has no word of advice to give, and constitutes Frick the Nero of
Homestead, consenting thereby to the employment of Pinkertons to
murder his old and trusted employees.

––––––

The Homestead slaughter of workingmen must serve to remind
the armies of labor of what is in store for them if the Carnegies, the
Phippses and the Fricks can, by the aid of the Pinkertons, come out
victorious.

Debs never let Labor forget Homestead. In a speech before an
Industrial Workers of the World convention at the Grand Central Palace
in New York City on December 10, 1905, he recalled Carnegie and
Homestead when he drew a distinction between capitalists and wage
earners. Carnegie had at this time been retired for five years and no
longer controlled the steel empire he had built, but Debs still identified
him as the archetype of the exploitative capitalist.

The capitalists, who own the tools that the working class use,
appropriate to themselves what the working class produce, and
this accounts for the fact that a few capitalists become fabulously
rich while the toiling millions remain in poverty, ignorance and
dependence.

Let me make this point perfectly clear for the benefit of those
who have not thought it out for themselves. Andrew Carnegie is a

type of the capitalist class. He owns the tools with which steel is produced. These tools are used by many thousands of working-men. Andrew Carnegie, who owns these tools, has absolutely nothing to do with the production of steel. He may be in Scotland, or where he will, the production of steel goes forward just the same. His mills at Pittsburgh, Duquesne and Homestead, where these tools are located, are thronged with thousands of toolless wage workers, who work day and night, in winter's cold and summer's heat, who endure all the privations and make all the sacrifices of health and limb and life, producing thousands upon thousands of tons of steel, yet not having an interest, even the slightest, in the product, and the workers, in exchange for their labor power, receive a wage that serves to keep them in producing order; and the more industrious they are, and the more they produce, the worse they are off; for the sooner they have produced more than Carnegie can get rid of in the markets, the tool houses are shut down and the workers are locked out in the cold.

In 1914 a force of armed men hired by the Rockefeller Fuel and Iron Company fired upon and burned out of their homes a community of protesting miners in Ludlow, Colorado. Two women and eleven children died in the fire. In an article for the *International Socialist Review* that year, Debs compared the actions at Ludlow to those at Homestead, an event that was still fresh in his memory even though nearly a quarter of a century had passed.

> The twenty-two years which lie between Homestead and Ludlow embrace a series of bloody and historic battles in the class war in the United States.
>
> The battle between the organized steel workers and the Carnegie-Pinkerton thugs which stirred the whole nation occurred on July 1, 1892; the Rockefeller massacre at Ludlow, which shocked the world, on April 20, 1914.
>
> In recalling Homestead I have been struck by the similarity of methods employed there and at Ludlow to crush the strikers, and by some other features common to both that have suggested a review of Homestead in the light of Ludlow, that we may the better understand their historic connection and at the same time see Ludlow in the light of Homestead.
>
> ———
>
> Andrew Carnegie incarnated triumphant and despotic capitalism at Homestead in July, 1892, just as John D. Rockefeller did at Ludlow in April, 1914.
>
> Carnegie, reducing the wages of the 4,000 employees in his steel mills from 15 to 40 percent, transforming his mills into forts, with

300 Pinkerton hirelings armed with Winchester rifles in command, fled to his castle in Scotland to escape the storm about to break. In vain was he appealed to by the whole country to cable the word that would end the bloody conflict, exactly as John D. Rockefeller, twenty-two years later, refused to utter the word that would have prevented the massacre at Ludlow.

That was and is Carnegie, who, with Rockefeller, is famed as a philanthropist, but whom history will pillory as cold-blooded murderers.

Homestead will haunt Carnegie and Ludlow will damn Rockefeller to the last hour of their lives and the memory of their basely murdered victims will load their names with infamy to the end of time.

It was in 1889, after he had become a plutocrat, that Carnegie began to write and preach about the "Gospel of Wealth," which was being exploited as oracular wisdom and as the quintessence of philanthropy by the grovelling and sycophantic capitalist press, purely because it was the gush and outpouring of a pompous plutocrat.

––––––

Carnegie used an army of Pinkerton hirelings and Rockefeller an army of Baldwin-Feltz thugs. The only difference was that at Homestead, twenty-two years ago, the plutocrats had not yet learned how to murder pregnant women and roast babes to death in the exemplification of their "Gospel of Wealth."

Debs helped see to it that Homestead haunted Carnegie for the rest of his days.

"MUCKRAKER" HAMLIN GARLAND'S EXPOSE IN *MCCLURE'S*

The Progressives who challenged big business after the turn of the twentieth century found much of the ammunition for their assault on men like Carnegie in the work of literary "realists" and journalistic "muckrakers." Two prominent realists were Franks Norris, whose novel *The Octopus* exposed the corruption of the railroads, and Upton Sinclair, whose novel *The Jungle* mercilessly described the health hazards of meat processing plants. President Roosevelt gave the muckrakers their name when he compared writers busy exposing industrial abuses to a figure in John Bunyan's classic moral tale *The Pilgrim's Progress,* a man who spent his time raking garbage. Roosevelt, who at times frowned on the muckrakers' work, was nevertheless himself influenced by their findings to become a modest reformer. Among the writers who raked up muck were Ida Tarbell, who wrote about the Standard Oil Trust, and Lincoln Steffens, who exposed the abuses of big city political machines. Both of them wrote their stories for *McClure's Magazine,* as did novelist and social commentator Hamlin Garland, who wrote the most damning indictment of the Carnegie Steel Corporation's actions in the Homestead crisis. In the following selection, "Homestead and Its Perilous Trades," from the June 1894, edition of *McClure's,* Garland described what he found when he visited Homestead a year after the bloodshed.

A cold, thin October rain was falling as I took the little ferry-boat and crossed the Monongahela River to see Homestead and its iron-mills. The town, infamously historic already, sprawled over the irregular hillside, circled by the cold gray river. On the flats close to the water's edge there were masses of great sheds, out of which grim smoke-stacks rose with a desolate effect, like the black stumps of a burned forest of great trees. Above them dense clouds of sticky smoke rolled heavily away.

Higher up the tenement-houses stood in dingy rows, alternating with vacant lots. Higher still stood some Queen Anne cottages, toward which slender sidewalks climbed like goat paths.

The streets of the town were horrible; the buildings were poor; the sidewalks were sunken, swaying, and full of holes, and the crossings were sharp-edged set like rocks in a river bed. Everywhere the yellow mud of the street lay kneaded into a sticky mass, through which groups of pale, lean men slouched in faded garments, grimy with the soot and grease of the mills.

———

The Carnegie mills stood down near the river at some distance from the ferry landing, and thither I took my way through the sticky yellow mud and the gray falling rain. I had secured for my guide a young man whose life had been passed in Homestead and who was quite familiar with the mills and workmen. I do not think he overstated the hardships of the workmen, whose duties he thoroughly understood. He spoke frankly and without undue prejudice of the management and the work.

We entered the yard through the fence which was aggrandized into a stockade during the riots of a year ago. We were in the yard of the "finished beams." On every side lay thousands of tons of iron. There came toward us a group of men pushing a cart laden with girders for building. They were lean men, pale and grimy. The rain was falling upon them. They wore a look of stoical indifference, though one or two of the younger fellows were scuffling as they pushed behind the car.

Farther on was heard the crashing thunder of falling iron plates, the hoarse coughing of great engines, and the hissing of steam.

Suddenly through the gloom I caught sight of the mighty up-soaring of saffron and sapphire flame, which marked the draught of the furnace of the Bessemer steel plant far down toward the water. It was a magnificent contrast to the dusky purple of the great smoky roofs below.

The great building which we entered first was a beam mill, "one of the finest in the world," my guide said. It was an immense shed, open at the sides, and filled with a mixed and intricate mass of huge machinery. On every side tumultuous action seemed to make every inch of ground dangerous. Savage little engines went rattling about among piles of great beams. Dimly on my left were huge engines, moving with thunderous pounding.

Garland described the "howl of horrible saws, the deafening hiss of escaping steam" as he was led through the work area. He was particularly troubled by the heat in which the men had to work as they turned iron ore into steal beams. Yet even as he pitied them, he admired their skill and fortitude.

I watched the men as they stirred the deeps beneath. I could not help admiring the swift and splendid action of their bodies. They had the silence and certainty one admires in the tiger's action. I dared not move for fear of flying metal, the swift swing of a crane, or the sudden lurch of a great carrier. The men could not look out for me. They worked with a sort of desperate attention and alertness.

"That looks like hard work," I said to one of them to whom my companion introduced me. He was breathing hard from his work.

"Hard! I guess it's hard. I lost forty pounds the first three months I came into this business. It sweats the life out of a man. I often drink two buckets of water during twelve hours; the sweat drips through my sleeves, and runs down my legs and fills my shoes."

"But that isn't the worst of it," said my guide; "it's a dog's life. Now, those men work twelve hours, and sleep and eat out ten more. You can see a man don't have much time for anything else. You can't see your friends, or do anything but work. That's why I got out of it. I used to come home so exhausted, staggering like a man with a 'jag.' It ain't any place for a sick man—is it, Joe?"

Joe was a tall young fellow, evidently an assistant at the furnace. He smiled. "It's all the work I want, and I'm no chicken—feel that arm."

I felt his arm. It was like a billet of steel. His abdomen was like a sheet of boiler iron. The hair was singed from his hands and arms by the heat of the furnace.

"The tools I handle weight one hundred and fifty pounds, and four o'clock in August they weight about a ton."

"What do you eat?"

"I have a bucket of 'grub'; I eat when I can. We have no let-up for eating. This job I'm on now isn't so bad as it might be, for we're running easy; but when we're running full, it's all I can stand."

———

Everywhere in this enormous building [the boiler-plate mill] were pits like the mouth of hell, and fierce ovens giving off a glare of heat, and burning wood and iron, giving off horrible stanches of gases. Thunder upon thunder, clang upon clang, glare upon glare! Torches flamed far up in the dark spaces above. Engines moved to and fro, and steam hissed and threatened.

Everywhere were grimy men with sallow and lean faces. The work was of the inhuman sort that hardens and coarsens.

"How long do you work?" I asked of a young man who stood at the furnace near me.

"Twelve hours," he replied. "The night set go on at six at night and come off at six in the morning. I go on at six and off at six."

"For how much pay?"

"Two dollars and a quarter."

"How much do those men get shovelling there in the rain?"

"One dollar and forty cents." (A cut has since taken place.)

"What proportion of the men get that pay?"

"Two-thirds of the whole plant, nearly two thousand. There are thirty-five hundred men in the mills. They get all prices, of course, from a dollar and forty cents up to the tonnage men, who get five and ten dollars per day when the mills run smooth."

"I suppose not many men make ten dollars per day."

"Well, hardly." He smiled. "Of course the 'rollers' and the 'heaters' get the most, but there are only two 'rollers' to each mill, and three 'heaters,' and they are responsible for their product. The most of the men get under two dollars per day."

"And it is twelve hours' work without stop?"

"You bet! And then again you see we only get this pay part of the time. The mills are liable to be shut down part of the year. They shut down part of the night sometimes, and of course we're docked. Then, again, the tendency of the proprietors is to cut down the tonnage men; that is, the 'rollers' and 'heaters' are now paid by the ton, but they'll some day be paid by the day, like the rest of us."

"You bet they will," said my guide. . . .

———

Upon such toil rests the splendor of American civilization.

———

. . . high above them in the tumult, an engine backed up with a load of crude molten iron, discharged into the converter, and the soaring saffron and orange and sapphire flames began again.

"Yes, the men call this the death-trap," repeated my guide, as we stood in the edge of the building; "they wipe a man out here every little while."

"In what way does death come?" I asked.

"Oh, all kinds of ways. Sometimes a chain breaks, and a ladle tips over, and the iron explodes—like that." He pointed at the newly emptied retort, out of which the drippings fell into the water which lay beneath like pools of green gold. As it fell, each drop exploded in a dull report.

"Sometimes the slag falls on the workmen from that roadway up there. Of course, if everything is working all smooth and a man watches out, why, all right! But you take it after they've been on duty twelve hours without sleep, and running like hell, everybody tired and loggy, and it's a different story."

My guide went on:

"You take it back in the beam mill—you saw how the men have to scatter when the carriers or the cranes move—well, sometimes they don't get out of the way; the men who should give warnings don't do it quick enough."

"What do those men get who are shovelling slag up there?"

"Fourteen cents an hour. If they worked eight hours, like a carpenter, they'd get one dollar and twelve cents."

"So a man works in peril of his life for fourteen cents an hour," I remarked.

"That's what he does. It ain't the only business he does it in, though."

"No," put in a young villager, who was looking on like ourselves. "A man'll do most anything to live."

————

"The wonder to me is, you don't all die of exposure and the changes of heat and cold."

My guide looked serious. "You don't notice any old men here." He swept his hand about the building. "It shortens life, just like mining; there is no question about that. That, of course, doesn't enter into the usual statement. But the long hours, the strain, and the sudden changes of temperature use a man up. He quits before he gets fifty. I can see lots of fellows here who are failing. They'll lay down in a few years. I went all over that, and I finally came to the decision that I'd peddle groceries rather than kill myself at this business."

"Well, what is the compensation? I mean, why do men keep on?"

"Oh, the common hands do it because they need a job, I suppose, and fellows like Joe expect to be one of the high-paid men."

"How much would that be per year?"

"Oh, three thousand or possibly four thousand a year."

"Does that pay for what it takes out of you?"

"No, I don't think it does," he confessed. "Still, a man has got to go into something."

———

"How do you stand on the late strike?" I asked another man.

"It's all foolishness; you can't do anything that way. The tonnage men brought it on; they could afford to strike, but we couldn't. The men working for less than two dollars can't afford to strike.

"'While capital wastes, labor starves,'" I ventured to quote.

"That's the idea; we can't hurt Carnegie by six months' starving. It's *our* ribs that'll show through our shirts."

"The strikes do not originate among the men of lowest pay?"

"No; a man working for fourteen cents an hour hasn't got any surplus for a strike."

———

I ate breakfast the next morning with two of the men I had seen the evening before. There was little of grace or leisurely courtesy in their actions. Their hearts were good, but their manners were those of ceaseless toilers. They resembled a Western threshing crew in all but their pallor.

"The worst part of the whole business is this," said one of them, as I was about saying good-by. "It brutalizes a man. You can't help it. You start in to be a man, but you become more and more a machine, and pleasures are few and far between. It's like any severe labor. It drags you down mentally and morally, just as it does physically. I wouldn't mind it so much if it weren't for the long hours. Many a trade would be all right if the hours could be shortened. Twelve hours is too long."

Again I boarded the little ferry and crossed the Monongahela on my way to the East. Out of those grim chimneys the belching smoke rose, defiling the cool, sweet air. Through this greenish-purple cloud the sun, red and large, glowed like an ingot of steel rising from a pit, filling the smoke with flushes of beautiful orange and rose amid the blue. The river was azure and burning gold, and the sun threw the most glorious shadows behind the smoke. Beyond lay the serene hills, a deeper purple.

Under the glory of gold and purple I heard the grinding howl of the iron-saws, and the throbbing, ferocious roar of the furnaces. The ferry-boat left a wake of blue that shone like the neck of a dove; and over the hills swept a fresh, moist wind. In the midst of God's bright morning, beside the beautiful river, the town and its industries lay like a cancer on the breast of a human body.

HISTORIANS LOUIS HACKER
AND JOSEPH WALL EVALUATE HOMESTEAD

The two men who have spent the most time examining Homestead in its historical context are Louis Morton Hacker and Joseph Wall. In his book, *The World of Andrew Carnegie*, Hacker took a close look at the Amalgamated Iron and Steel union, Carnegie's feelings about unions and collective bargaining in general, and his culpability in the Homestead incident.

It [Amalgamated] had organized only the skilled workers. Its national officers sought to negotiate for all the workers of Homestead. At the same time, the heaters, rollers, puddlers were determined to maintain their privileged position when their skills were no longer at the basis of steel's growth and changing character. As Frick wrote to Carnegie: "The mills have never been able to turn out the product they should, owing to being held back by the Amalgamated men." In fact, the Amalgamated had deported itself like a medieval guild, insisting that its monopoly hold over its jobs at Homestead be respected. The Irish controlled the Bessemer and open-hearth furnaces; the Welsh, the rolling mills. When vacancies appeared, the Amalgamated made its own replacements, sending back to Britain for substitute workers. Even more; its work rules in 1892 forbade the training of apprentices, limited the output of its members, and even prescribed the quality of pig iron to be used and the proportions of other materials entering into the mix.

To Carnegie himself, this was "feudalism," but his own paternalism—that "capital and labor" were partners—offered few realistic solutions in a complex situation where justice may have been on the company's side, but which demanded a willingness to compromise and to make concessions, for humanity's sake if for nothing else. Thus—and here were all the elements of a tragedy—the unskilled, those largely recruited by Frick from the "new immigration," were as much the victims of Amalgamated tyranny (they could not be trained for and moved into better jobs) as they were of Frick's hard labor policies.

They were undoubtedly hard. Steady wages were probably higher than elsewhere in the industry, but certainly low, as far as the maintenance of decent standards of living were concerned. The unskilled lived wretchedly in their "Hunkyvilles" in the river bottom, where houses had no running water and no sanitation facilities. The twelve-hour day (and Frick's speed-up) led to fatigue and a heavy toll of industrial accidents and deaths. The newcomers did not like the older immigrants; but they liked Frick less—-and they went out on strike when the Amalgamated Association did.

Did Carnegie mean to crush the union? He quit the country in
the spring of 1892—as had been his custom for many years—leaving Frick in charge of the company, for he had been made its chairman in 1889. Before going, Carnegie had issued a statement
declaring that Homestead was to be nonunion, but then he had
withdrawn it. What orders did he leave Frick? Certainly he had written Frick, as he had written Abbott three years before [at the last
contract negotiation], that in the event of a strike there was to be a
complete shutdown—and no scabs. Frick was to tell the workers:
"'Until a majority vote (secret ballot) to go to work, have a good
time; when a majority vote to start, start it is!' I am satisfied that the
employer or firm who gets the reputation of adhering to that will
never have a prolonged stoppage, or much ill feeling."
     On this crucial matter Frick insisted he had disagreed; he had
argued for running the plant in the event of a strike—in short, for a
showdown with the union. Carnegie had not challenged Frick; he
had left no positive orders, and in consequence Carnegie's culpability cannot be denied. When Frick, therefore, refused to meet with
the union spokesmen a second time and in effect issued an ultima-
tum to them, he meant that thenceforth he was not going to brook
the union's intervention. This was union-busting; and Carnegie's
silence on this point, too, meant acceptance.

Joseph Wall, the historian who provided such a thorough assessment of Carnegie as an industrial tycoon, also addressed Carnegie's
part in Homestead.

> . . . Carnegie was torn between two desires: to reduce labor costs
> to a level competitive with rival steel manufacturers and, at the
> same time, to appear before the world as America's most enlight-
> ened and progressive employer of a mass labor force. Because there
> was no easy way to reconcile these two contradictory policies, crit-
> ics have often raised the cry of hypocrisy against Carnegie, charging
> him with preaching one doctrine while practising quite another.

―――

> If Carnegie could have subscribed wholeheartedly to Frick's posi-
> tion [to use workmen at the lowest cost] he would have saved him-
> self a great deal of anguish and would have avoided the epithet of
> hypocrite that was to be hurled at him by both contemporary crit-
> ics and later historians. To call Carnegie a hypocrite in his labor poli-
> cy as stated in theory and as put into practice is too easy. For such a
> charge leaves unanswered the question of why Carnegie found it
> necessary to propound the doctrines that he did in the age in
> which he lived. No one expected the late-nineteenth-century indus-
> trialist to provide labor with a Bill of Rights. Frick, not Carnegie, was

the norm, and to deviate from that norm was to ask for trouble. Then what compelled Carnegie to write his two remarkable essays for *Forum* magazine in 1886? Why had he gone out of his way to spell out a policy which could not fail later to embarrass him and make him vulnerable to the charge of hypocrisy?

To answer these questions requires a far more profound insight into Carnegie's personality and career than the simple charge of hypocrisy can provide. In part, the answer lies in Carnegie's vanity, in his desire to be loved and admired by all Americans. A special drawer in his big roll-top desk was labeled "Gratitude and sweet words," and it was one of the tasks of his personal secretary to clip out any flattering notice of Carnegie that appeared in the public press and to file it in this drawer for Carnegie's later perusal and enjoyment. And in part, the answer may be found in the ability of Captain Jones to convince him that an enlightened labor policy was good business practice, and that his two basic desires, to make money and to be a kind and good employer, were not antithetical, but rather complementary. A well-rested, well-paid, highly trained employee could produce twice as much with far less waste of raw materials than an under-paid, over-worked, ignorant peasant brought over from the steppes of eastern Russia. Jones's favorite workers were what he called "'Buckwheats'—young American boys judiciously mixed" in their ethnic background. As long as Jones remained the dominant figure in the Carnegie steel mills, his influence prevailed in labor policy. [Jones died in a mill explosion before Homestead, and Frick became Carnegie's major assistant.]

But, above all, the answer lies in Carnegie's lifelong quest to reconcile the Radical egalitarianism of his Dunfermline childhood with the capitalistic success that he enjoyed in manhood. For his own peace of mind he had to believe that he had not betrayed the faith of his fathers when he became a multimillionaire and an employer of tens of thousands of men. He once wrote that of all the lines in Robert Burns's poems he loved, the one that meant the most to him was "Thine own reproach alone do fear." Indeed, Carnegie was so confident of his own abilities that it was the only reproach he *could* fear. But fear it he did, and somehow he had to justify his kind of life to himself. . . .

Whether Homestead was an unfortunate mistake, an exception to the way the Carnegie did business, or merely one example of his general abuse of labor, the events of July 1892, will always be linked to Carnegie's empire. He knew this was true, and he hated it, but nothing ever removed from him what he considered a single stain and others called the dye of his wool.

DREW LEWIS ON BREAKING
THE AIR TRAFFIC CONTROLLER'S STRIKE

Labor unions gained strength during the twentieth century, especially after 1933, when they were given protection and encouragement by the administration of Franklin D. Roosevelt. There were still many strikes and even a few violent confrontations, when labor and management did not see eye to eye; but rarely did the battles escalate to the level of Homestead. Perhaps one reason for this was that the labor force steadily became more "white collar," more the kind of people who worked in offices rather than factories, people not as financially desperate as the men of the Carnegie works, not as prone to settle disputes with physical force. Nevertheless, there have been cases of lockouts and wholesale firings by intractable managers, and strikes have continued to be broken to this day.

One strike was broken in the late summer of 1981, and the "owner" who broke it by firing all the strikers was the U. S. government. For most of that year the Professional Air Traffic Controllers Association (PATCO) tried to negotiate with the Reagan administration for a new contract. They asked for a $10,000 a year across the board pay raise, better retirement benefits, and reduction of working hours from forty to thirty-two per week. Leaders and members alike said the most important demand was the latter, that the pressures under which they worked called for fewer hours, that this reduction would make them more effective in handling the life and death details of their work. From the beginning of negotiations, Secretary of Transportation Drew Lewis refused PATCO's demands and argued that since the workers were vital to the nation's safety *and* employed by the federal government, they had no right to strike.

On August 3, 1981, almost 13,000 air traffic controllers went on strike. They were told to return to work immediately or be terminated. At the end of 48 hours, the seventy percent still on strike were fired. PATCO requested amnesty for these workers. Lewis and Reagan refused. Moe Biller, president of the Postal Workers Union, said the United States was "the only democracy in the world that sentences its government workers to 'economic capital punishment'" for daring to strike for better conditions refused them by the government. He pointed out that there can be no true bargaining without the power to withhold labor. But Drew Lewis, acting and speaking for a silent president, did not budge. In response to a question posed by *U.S. News and World Report* (August 24, 1981) as to why he would not grant the workers amnesty and let them return to work pending further discussions, he spoke in the tradition of Henry Clay Frick. Circumstances were a bit different, but the results for the striking workers were the same.

The issue is more basic than that. These people signed an oath to support the Constitution of the United States and not to strike against the federal government, because their jobs affected safety and the public welfare.

Now we're in a position that the very core of this democracy—the very system of law that we've developed over the last 200 years—is in jeopardy. The President has to support the Constitution and cannot be in a position of permitting these people—a few people in a country of more than 200 million—to blatantly violate the law while expecting other people to support the law.

———

. . . There's no possibility that we're going to renegotiate now with people who are on strike, who have walked off the job, who are out there picketing, tearing up their termination notices and violating statutes and orders of the federal courts. We cannot do it.

———

First of all, we found out when the strike began that we have about 3,000 more controllers than we really need. There are another 3,000 people whose jobs are fundamentally clerical in nature—answering telephones, filling out forms.

Second, the controllers were only spending about 4½ hours a day on the radarscopes. The rest of the time went for lunch breaks, coffee breaks or other relief periods they wanted.

Third, let's not forget that we have 3,000 supervisors and military controllers, so that our total complement of people—8,800—is close to 75 percent of the normal weekly requirement.

Finally, think of the air lines as you would an expressway going in and out of a city. When it's at 100 percent of capacity, the expressway is bumper to bumper. When it's at 75 percent of capacity, cars move freely. It's the same in the airways. When the airways are not crowded, it is a very simple system to move and control the airplanes. It's that last 5 or 10 percent of capacity that, along with bad weather, gets planes stacked up. So we are in a position, with considerably reduced staff, to operate this system very safely at 75 percent capacity.

The strike was broken. The terminated personnel were never rehired. Reagan's popularity declined only slightly at the end of his first year in office and that due not to the way PATCO personnel were treated but rather to his plans to alter Social Security. Polls showed that

65% of the public approved of the harsh actions against PATCO; and the White House announced that its mail on the issue ran 1,000:1 in favor of Lewis' action. During the year-end discussion with reporters about the year 1981, Reagan did not mention the incident, and no reporter bothered to ask about it.

QUESTIONS FOR CRITICAL EXAMINATION

1. After reading his description of how he dealt with his workmen, what conclusions can be drawn about Carnegie's attitude toward labor? What were his strengths and weaknesses when dealing with workers? To what extent was he, after he became wealthy, able to understand and communicate with the working class?

2. How did Carnegie structure the events of the Homestead strike to excuse himself from blame for the violence? Whom did he hold responsible for the trouble, and whom did he avoid blaming? What impression of Homestead would you have if you only had Carnegie's side of the story?

3. What was the reaction of radicals such as the Emma Goldman's Anarchists to the Homestead uprising? What made them interpret it as a first step in a revolution? Why did Sasha feel so strongly that he had to go to Homestead, and why did he decide to target Henry Clay Frick?

4. What makes Debs' account of Homestead so powerful? What image of Carnegie emerges from his indictment? Show how Debs used colorful language to create good and evil characters in the drama and how he employed religious language to buttress his arguments.

5. What definitions of capitalism and capitalists did Debs give to his audiences? How did he use Homestead and Ludlow to prove his points? Why did he continually return to Carnegie and Homestead to illustrate his theories of class warfare?

6. By combining the assessments of Homestead by historians Hacker and Wall, what conclusions can you draw about what happened there and about Carnegie's part in it? To what degree did the conflicts in Carnegie's philosophy of labor and management lead to the bloody confrontation?

7. How were the Homestead and PATCO strikes alike, and how were they different? Why did Drew Lewis feel he had to deny both the demands of PATCO and amnesty to the strikers? Why were the majority of Americans happy with the termination of the controllers? What does this say about late twentieth century America?

Chapter Five

___

THE CONSPICUOUS PHILANTHROPIST: ANDREW CARNEGIE AS AMERICAN SAINT

> "The man who dies thus rich dies disgraced."
>
> ANDREW CARNEGIE
> *"Wealth,"* North American Review, 1889

Andrew Carnegie's life demonstrates the complexity of human nature. He was the American success story *par excellence,* the fulfillment of the American dream. He would be remembered today for his rise from poverty to riches, for being a captain of industry, for being at one point in history the richest man in the world. Yet it was another achievement, in some ways the most impressive, which has left the strongest lasting impression on the collective American memory: his philanthropy. Even before he concluded his life of financial acquisition and retired to his life of distribution, he had tentatively begun to give his fortune away. He started by making donations to his home town of Dunfermline; and then in his mill towns Braddock, Duquesne, and Homestead he built social centers that housed libraries, class rooms, gymnasiums, and swimming pools. Men who worked at the plants, their wives, and their children could use the libraries free of charge and the other facilities for small fees.

In 1889, with his article on "Wealth," later called "The Gospel of Wealth," he publicly proclaimed the responsibility of the rich man to give his money away. It was after his retirement at age 65, however, that he devoted himself full time to his philanthropy. Although he remained to his death nineteen years later a rich man, with mansions in New York City, Scotland, and rural Massachusetts, he succeeded over those two decades in giving away the $300,000,000 he had been paid for his empire in 1900, plus the interest it had earned. That would be in today's exchange well over five billion dollars.

ROBBER BARON CARNEGIE
BECOMES A PHILANTHROPIST

Carnegie reached the age of 65 with mixed feelings about the financial empire he had built. As with most people accustomed to being in charge of a large enterprise, he hated to give it up; and he knew that inevitably his corporation would change under new leadership. He hated to see it run by the new kind of bosses, men he feared were more Frick than Carnegie, men who might well permit more Homestead fiascos or let it be unionized into incompetence. On the other hand, he had other plans for the remainder of his life. He wanted to read and write. He wanted to speak out for worthy causes such as world peace, which he believed must be maintained if the industrial world wanted to avoid self-destruction; and against the growing spirit of American imperialism, which he said would replace "triumphant democracy" with "triumphant despotism." Most importantly he wanted to give much of his fortune away in the most effective and impressive way possible.

To give away his wealth would be to exorcize a demon. As early as 1868 he wrote (as quoted in Matthew Josephson, *The Robber Barons,* p. 106),". . . The amassing of wealth is one of the worst species of idolatry—no idol more debasing than the worship of money." In the article "Wealth" he wrote,"The man who dies rich, thus dies disgraced." He did not want to leave an immense fortune to heirs (until 1897 he had no children) because he considered inherited wealth an occasion for sloth. He even wrote that he favored governmental imposition of high inheritance taxes to prevent the establishment of a wealthy leisure class. While his retirement package left his partners and his brother Thomas's family wealthy, while he and his wife and daughter lived in luxury on the several millions he kept for himself, he did indeed give most of his fortune away.

The opportunity to "sell out" and start a "life of the mind" came in 1901. The financier J. P. Morgan made overtures to buy the Carnegie

Political cartoon: Money Bags & Wheat Pit with Andrew Carnegie and John W. Gates. "To Die Rich Is to Die Disgraced." John W. Gates—"You will have your wish if you try Chicago wheat." Undated.

mills in order to form a corporation that would hold a monopoly over the production of steel in the United States. The nine years since Homestead had seen his steel mills make their greatest profits, and Carnegie replied to Morgan that he believed his empire had a market value of $492,000,000, of which $300,000,000 was his alone. Without haggling Morgan agreed to these terms and arranged the purchase, combining the Carnegie holdings with other smaller ones to form United States Steel, at the time of consolidation the first corporation to be worth over a billion dollars. When Morgan shook hands with Carnegie to seal the transaction, he congratulated him on being the "richest man in the world." Later Carnegie told Morgan that he should have asked for $100,000,000 more, and Morgan assured him that he would have received it.

The new corporation printed out $300,000,000 in bonds for Carnegie, which he placed in an account separate from the thirty million dollars already in his name. He spent the next eighteen years giving it away, living on his own private fortune. In doing so he at least partially exorcized his demonic idol, money, and did not die as disgraced as he might have done had he kept it all, at least not in his own eyes. He could always tell himself that he was indeed a liberal, a democrat, a Chartist, a friend of the working class, not the ogre of inhumane industrialism, not the "coward" of Homestead.

His love of reading, which he believed was the key to success in life, led him to his first and perhaps still his most notable philanthropic endeavor, the building of libraries. He never forgot old Colonel Anderson, the man who opened his library for boys like Carnegie to use for self-improvement; and in building libraries he believed he was repaying the debt he owed him. His grants of money built 2,811 libraries: 1,946 of them in the United States, 660 in Britain and Ireland, 156 in Canada, 23 in New Zealand, 13 in South Africa, 6 in the British West Indies, 4 in Australia, and one in each of three Pacific island colonies. The total cost for these libraries was $50,364,808, $44,853,731 of it spent in the United States. Every state except Rhode Island got at least one Carnegie library, and most of them were located in the American Midwest. He never asked that any library be named for him, although he was pleased when most of them were. He kept tight control over architectural designs, favoring what might be called British Empire style; but his only requirement of the municipality requesting and receiving the grants was that it supply the building with books and keep the property in good repair at a cost of one-tenth the grant per year. After some griping, most of the towns accepted his offers and named the libraries for him. Not all lived up to their promise to match the amount of the grant within ten years, and not all the libraries lasted longer than the ten years.

He also set up the Carnegie Relief Fund, $4,000,000 to provide pensions and health programs for his former employees in the twelve plants he had owned. Any employee who had reached the age of sixty years, had been at least fifteen years continuously in the service of the company, and was incapacitated, might be pensioned. Someone under sixty who became permanently disabled from sickness or injuries received on the job might also, if his case fulfilled the foregoing requirements, be pensioned.

Carnegie bought and gave 4,100 organs to various churches. He founded the Carnegie Trust, which supported Scottish, English, and Irish universities; Carnegie institutes of technology in Pittsburgh and Washington for the promotion of scientific research and training; and Carnegie Hall for the performing arts in New York. The Carnegie Foundation, with an initial endowment of $125,000,000, has for a century supported programs to improve teaching; and a fund was established to provide pensions for members of the academic professions, which led to the modern pension program TIAA-CREF. A pacifist since early manhood, he contributed $10,000,000 toward the creation the Carnegie Endowment for International Peace and building the Peace Palace, a courthouse and library, at the World Court in The Hague. In 1911 he created the Carnegie Corporation, whose function it was to fund worthy causes that he knew would arise in the future.

His philanthropic endeavors proved to be a full-time job. In a letter to the editor of the newspaper *The Independent* in 1913, he wrote, "Pity the poor millionaire, for the way of the millionaire is hard," referring to the work load and frustrations of philanthropy. He actually felt that philanthropy was harder work than creating a financial empire. Yet he reveled in this last phase of his career. Near the end of his life he asked his private secretary, "How much did you say I had given away, Poynton?" When Poynton answered, "$324,657,399," Carnegie said, "Good heavens! Where did I ever get all that money?" There was a gleam in his eye, both for the amount he had made and the amount he had given away.

World War I hit the pacifist Carnegie hard. He considered war of any kind destructive, and this war between industrialized nations was certain to be devastating to all. He supported Democrat Woodrow Wilson in the 1912 presidential election because he feared the more belligerent Theodore Roosevelt might lead the nation into a foolhardy military adventure. Having contributed large sums to Princeton University while Wilson was its president, he felt he might exert pacifistic influences on the scholarly politician. Carnegie may have indeed, through his calls for a "League of Peace" to settle differences between nations, have influenced Wilson's dream of a postwar League of Nations to prevent future wars. When war came in 1914, Carnegie began urging Wilson to arbitrate a peace between Britain and Germany; but by 1917 he agreed with Wilson that his adopted country should enter the war.

Because during the war it was unsafe to travel the North Atlantic, he was never able to visit Scotland again; and he spent his last years at his New York City mansion and at Shadowbrook, his lakeside home near Lenox, Massachusetts. There on August 11, 1919, three months short of his eighty-fifth birthday, he died, leaving his widow Louise and his recently married twenty-two-year-old daughter Margaret. Although he was not a church member, a Presbyterian minister delivered his eulogy before a small group of friends, and he was buried privately in the Sleepy Hollow Cemetery in Tarrytown, New York. His grave was

Andrew Carnegie's private library in his 66-room residence in New York City.

marked by a Celtic cross, cut from stone quarried at Skibo in Scotland. He died rich but only 10% as rich as he could have died had he kept all his wealth. Five years later, Samuel Gompers, a founder and head of the American Federation of Labor, which Carnegie despised, was buried in an adjoining plot.

CARNEGIE'S PHILOSOPHY OF GIVING: *THE GOSPEL OF WEALTH*

Philanthropy is usually associated with religious sentiment. Love and care for one's fellow man is commonly believed to be based on the concept of God's love for mankind. It is therefore interesting to analyze Carnegie's religious philosophy. He was removed from traditional Scots Presbyterianism the day his father stormed out of that Sabbath sermon on infant damnation, based on the Calvinist doctrine of election, shouting, "If that be your God and your religion, I seek a new God and a new

religion." Although in Pittsburgh his father took him to Church of the
New Jerusalem services, where two righteous aunts hoped he would
become a minister; he was never convinced of Swedenborgianism. "As I
grew up there was no rest for me in Swedenborg," he later explained. He
did eventually find a "faith," but it was one of his own creation, not traditional or orthodox. It was a belief in the fundamentally positive thrust
of evolution. In the following passage from his memoirs, he recalled how
as a young man, after some years of searching, he finally came to embrace
the principles that sustained him through his long life.

> At this period of my life I was all at sea. No creed, no system,
> reached me. All was chaos. I had outgrown the old and had found
> no substitute. Carlyle's wrestlings will give you an idea of my condi-
> tion. Here came to me Spencer and Darwin, whom I read with
> absorbing interest, until laying down a volume one day I was able to
> say, "That settles the question." I had found at last the guides which
> led me to the temples of man's real knowledge upon earth. These
> works were revelations to me; here was the truth which reconciled
> all things as far as the infinite mind can grasp them, the alembic
> which harmonized hitherto conflicting ideas and brought order out
> of chaos; what the law of gravitation did for matter, the law of evolu-
> tion did for mind. I was upon firm ground, and with every year of
> my life since there has come less dogmatism, less theology, but
> greater reverence.

In a speech Carnegie prepared for his inaugural address as Rector
of St. Andrews University in Scotland in 1902, a speech which was
never delivered publicly because the regents considered it too secular,
too non-Christian for a Presbyterian institution, he gave the essence of
his religious faith. Theology, he intended to tell the academic body,
should be defined by progressive science.

> The truth which makes us free will keep us free only if we keep
> open minds and embrace it as the light brightens and we see more
> clearly that Revelation neither began nor ended with our Scriptures
> or our theology. New and mighty truths are yet to be revealed at
> intervals, and we are to see present truths more perfectly, probably
> to the end of time. There are more things in heaven and earth than
> are dreamt of today either in our philosophy or religion.
>   Your task is to elevate and improve your fellow-men; first, always
> by example, and, second, often by precept. Much of your influence
> for good will depend upon the ideal of highest manhood which you
> create for yourselves and pursue. The ideal man, as I have some-
> times tried to imagine him, is he, who although hoping for everlast-

ing existence with those he loves, yet concentrates his thoughts and efforts upon the duties of this life in which he has been placed, strictly obeys the judge within, doing right, avoiding wrong, neither for hope of reward nor fear of punishment, here or hereafter, but solely because his conscience tells him it is right or wrong—virtue being its own ample reward.

Carnegie was not a Christian. He combined a belief in the progress and enlightenment of science with a confidence in his own inner moral compass and fashioned a faith that satisfied his own needs. It is from this "faith" that his philanthropy came. In giving away $300,000,000, he not only brought the fruits of science and his love for learning to his fellow man but tried to clear his conscience of idolatry and the love of money, and to clear his name of the one great blot, Homestead.

A major step forward in his philanthropic endeavors—the step that caught the public's attention and brought him praise and spurred him on to fulfill his goals—was the article he wrote for the June 1889, edition of the *North American Review.* "Wealth" was his first attempt to explain how the man of riches should use his fortune. Coming as it did from one of America's richest men, it was an immediate sensation and was reprinted in several other periodicals. The British Prime Minister William Gladstone (a Scot such as Carnegie) recommended that it be published in the English journal *Pall Mall Budget,* and as earlier noted its editor William Snead suggested expanding the title to "The Gospel of Wealth." Later that year Carnegie wrote a follow-up article, answering questions raised by the first, titled "The Best Fields for Philanthropy." He added other articles to those two over the next decade, and in 1900 the group was published in a volume that became his most famous book, *The Gospel of Wealth.*

The following passage it taken from the original article "Wealth," where Carnegie first made public thoughts about money he had contemplated for several years. He began by explaining that he would be speaking not of moderate wealth, that which every man needs to support his family, but what he called surplus wealth.

There are but three modes in which surplus wealth can be disposed of. It can be left to the families of the decedents; or it can be bequeathed for public purposes; or, finally, it can be administered by its possessors during their lives. Under the first and second modes most of the wealth of the world that has reached the few has hitherto been applied. Let us in turn consider each of these modes. The first is the most injudicious. In monarchical countries, the estates and the greatest portion of the wealth are left to the first son, that the vanity of the parent may be gratified by the thought that his name and title are to descend unimpaired to succeeding generations. The condition of this class in Europe to-day teaches the failure of such hopes or ambitions. The successors have become impoverished through their follies, or from the fall in the value of land. Even in Great Britain the strict law of entail has been found inadequate to maintain an hereditary class. Its soil is rapidly passing into the hands of the stranger. Under republican institutions the division of property among the children is much fairer; but the question which forces itself upon thoughtful men in all lands is, Why should men leave great fortunes to their children? If this is done from affection, is it not misguided affection? Observation teaches that, generally speaking, it is not well for the children that they should be so burdened. Neither is it well for the State. Beyond providing for the wife and daughters moderate sources of income, and very moderate allowances indeed, if any, for the sons, men may well hesitate; for it is no longer questionable that great sums bequeathed often work more for the injury than for the good of the recipients. Wise men will soon conclude that, for the best interests of the members of their families, and of the State, such bequests are an improper use of their means.

———

As to the second mode, that of leaving wealth at death for public uses, it may be said that this is only a means for the disposal of wealth, provided a man is content to wait until he is dead before he becomes of much good in the world. Knowledge of the results of legacies bequeathed is not calculated to inspire the brightest hopes of much posthumous good being accomplished by them. The cases are not few in which the real object sought by the testator is not attained, nor are they few in which his real wishes are thwarted. In many cases the bequests are so used as to become only monuments of his folly. It is well to remember that it requires the exercise of not less ability than that which acquires it, to use wealth so as to be really beneficial to the community. Besides this, it may fairly be said that no man is to be extolled for doing what he cannot help doing, nor is he to be thanked by the community to which he only leaves wealth at death. Men who leave vast sums in this way may fairly be thought men who would not have left it at all had they been able to take it with them. The memories of such cannot be held in grateful remembrance, for there is no grace in their gifts. It is not to be wondered at that such bequests seem so generally to lack the blessing.

Carnegie then spoke favorably of the new death duties which states were beginning to impose on wealth. Of all taxation, he said, this was the wisest because it condemned "the selfish millionaire's unworthy life." The man with surplus wealth should be goaded into giving it for worthy projects or have it confiscated by the state when he died. Such taxes were then in the range of 10% of the estate, but Carnegie said it should be far more.

> There remains, then, only one mode of using great fortunes; but in this we have the true antidote for the temporary unequal distribution of wealth, the reconciliation of the rich and the poor—a reign of harmony, another ideal, differing, indeed, from that of the Communist in requiring only the further evolution of existing conditions, not the total overthrow of our civilization. It is founded upon the present most intense Individualism, and the race is prepared to put it in practice by degrees whenever it pleases. Under its sway we shall have an ideal State, in which the surplus wealth of the few will become, in the best sense, the property of the many, because administered for the common good; and this wealth, passing through the hands of the few, can be made a much more potent force for the elevation of our race than if distributed in small sums to the people themselves. Even the poorest can be made to see this, and to agree that great sums gathered by some of their fellow-citizens and spent for public purposes, from which the masses reap the principal benefit, are more valuable to them than if scattered among themselves in trifling amounts through the course of many years.

Then Carnegie discussed the public contributions of two millionaires, Peter Cooper who built New York's Cooper Institute, where working men could study and hear lectures, and Samuel Tilden who built the New York Public Library. It was much better for these two men to oversee construction of public institutions during their lifetimes than for the institutions to be built after their deaths, when they could not be sure they were done properly. It was also much better to provide such institutions for working men to improve themselves than to give the money to them in higher wages. Carnegie did not trust the working man to make the best cultural use of his income.

> Poor and restricted are our opportunities in this life, narrow our horizon, our best work most imperfect; but rich men should be thankful for one inestimable boon. They have it in their power during their lives to busy themselves in organizing benefactions from which the masses of their fellows will derive lasting advantage, and thus dignify their own lives. The highest life is probably to be

reached, not by such imitation of the life of Christ as Count Tolstoi gives us, but, while animated by Christ's spirit, by recognizing the changed conditions of this age, and adopting modes of expressing this spirit suitable to the changed conditions under which we live, still laboring for the good of our fellows, which was the essence of his life and teaching, but laboring in a different manner.

This, then, is held to be the duty of the man of wealth: To set an example of modest, unostentatious living, shunning display or extravagance; to provide moderately for the legitimate wants of those dependent upon him; and, after doing so, to consider all surplus revenues which come to him simply as trust funds, which he is called upon to administer, and strictly bound as a matter of duty to administer in the manner which, in his judgment, is best calculated to produce the most beneficial results for the community—the man of wealth thus becoming the mere trustee and agent for his poorer brethren, bringing to their service his superior wisdom, experience, and ability to administer, doing for them better than they would or could do for themselves.

———

In bestowing charity, the main consideration should be to help those who will help themselves; to provide part of the means by which those who desire to improve may do so; to give those who desire to rise the aids by which they may rise; to assist, but rarely or never to do all. Neither the individual nor the race is improved by almsgiving. Those worthy of assistance, except in rare cases, seldom require assistance. The really valuable men of the race never do....

———

. . . The best means of benefiting the community is to place within its reach the ladders upon which the aspiring can rise—free libraries, parks, and means of recreation, by which men are helped in body and mind; works of art, certain to give pleasure and improve the public taste; and public institutions of various kinds, which will improve the general condition of the people; in this manner returning their surplus wealth to the mass of their fellows in the forms best calculated to do them lasting good.

Thus is the problem of rich and poor to be solved. The laws of accumulation will be left free, the laws of distribution free. Individualism will continue, but the millionaire will be but a trustee for the poor, intrusted for a season with a great part of the increased wealth of the community, but administering it for the community far better than it could or would have done for itself. The best minds will thus have reached a stage in the development of the race in which it is clearly seen that there is no mode of disposing of surplus wealth creditable to thoughtful and earnest men into whose hands it flows, save by using it year by year for the general good. This day already dawns. Men may die without incurring the pity of their fellows, still sharers in great business enterprises from which their capital cannot be or has not been withdrawn, and which is left chiefly at death for public uses; yet the day is not far distant when the man who dies leaving behind him millions of available wealth, which was free to him to administer during life, will pass away "unwept, unhonored, and unsung," no matter to what uses he leaves the dross which he cannot take with him. Of such as these the public verdict will then be: "The man who dies thus rich dies disgraced."

Such, in my opinion is the true gospel concerning wealth, obedience to which is destined some day to solve the problem of the rich and the poor, and to bring "Peace on earth, among men good will."

In a follow-up article, published in the *North American Review* of December 1889, Carnegie listed "The Best Fields for Philanthropy." Men of wealth could found universities in the fashion of Stanford in California; they could build free public libraries after the pattern of Pratt in Baltimore; they could contribute to medical institutions as had Vanderbilt to the Columbia Medical School; they could build parks the way Mrs. Schenley had done in Pittsburgh; they could build civic halls, especially those where musical presentations could be held, such as the Springer Hall in Cincinnati; they could build public swimming pools and other recreational facilities; and they could contribute to churches. Carnegie admitted some concern about the last of these suggestions because he did not believe in encouraging sectarianism; but if gifts encouraged a certain type of religious activity, they were positive. In romantic imagery he described helping erect a simple sanctuary, used both for worship and civic lectures, where all groups could meet, "up whose sides the honeysuckle and columbine may climb, and from whose tower the sweet-tolling bell may sound."

Looking over this list it is possible to see the places where Carnegie would begin placing cash grants and where eventually he would invest most of his fortune. His philanthropy was based on a great deal of thought and consideration. He would contribute to educational, cultural, recreational, and even religious institutions, investing his wealth in ways that he believed encouraged personal growth and promoted the common good.

The man who builds a university, library, or laboratory performs no more useful work than he who elects to devote himself and his surplus means to the adornment of a park, the gathering together of a collection of pictures for the public, or the building of a memorial arch. These are all true laborers in the vineyard. The only point required by the gospel of wealth is that the surplus which accrues from time to time in the hands of a man should be administered by him in his own lifetime for that purpose which is seen by him, as trustee, to be best for the good of the people. To leave at death what he cannot take away, and place upon others the burden of the work which it was his duty to perform, is to do nothing worthy. This requires no sacrifice, nor any sense of duty to his fellows.

Time was when the words concerning the rich man entering the kingdom of heaven were regarded as a hard saying. To-day, when all questions are probed to the bottom and the standards of faith receive the most liberal interpretations, the startling verse has been relegated to the rear, to await the next kindly revision as one of those things which cannot be quite understood, but which, meanwhile, it is carefully to be noted, are not to be understood literally. But is it so very improbably that the next stage of thought is to restore the doctrine in all its pristine purity and force, as being in perfect harmony with sound ideas upon the subject of wealth and poverty, the rich and the poor, and the contrasts everywhere seen and deplored? In Christ's day, it is evident, reformers were against the wealthy. It is none the less evident that we are fast recurring to that position to-day; and there will be nothing to surprise the student of sociological development if society should soon approve the text which has caused so much anxiety: "It is easier for a camel to enter the eye of a needle than for a rich man to enter the kingdom of heaven." Even if the needle were the small casement at the gates, the words betoken serious difficulty for the rich. It will be but a step for the theologian from the doctrine that he who dies rich dies disgraced, to that which brings upon the man punishment or deprivation hereafter.

The gospel of wealth but echoes Christ's words. It calls upon the millionaire to sell all that he hath and give it in the highest and best form to the poor by administering his estate himself for the good of his fellows, before he is called upon to lie down and rest upon the bosom of Mother Earth. So doing, he will approach his end no longer the ignoble hoarder of useless millions; poor, very poor indeed, in money, but rich, very rich, twenty times a millionaire still, in the affection, gratitude, and admiration of his fellow-men, and—sweeter far—soothed and sustained by the still, small voice within, which, whispering, tells him that, because he has lived, perhaps one small part of the great world has been bettered just a little. This much is sure: against such riches as these no bar will be found at the gates of Paradise.

Carnegie Library of Pittsburgh.

*Cartoon of Carnegie the philanthropist as
a stained glass "Saint Andrew."*

CARNEGIE'S PHILANTHROPY
IN THE AMERICAN POPULAR IMAGINATION

Someone of Carnegie's prominence made news with everything he did;
and had he given away only a fraction of what he contributed to public
projects, he would have made an impression on the American mind. The
fact that he gave away 90% of his wealth, and that it amounted to over

$300,000,000, made an exceedingly deep impression. He was not the first American philanthropist, and since his time others have given away more, but no other fabulously wealthy person has given so great a portion of his wealth away. People came to admire him as much for his philanthropy as for his rise to riches and his mid-career power and wealth. During the last two decades of his life he was most often described as a "saintly" figure.

POPULAR RESPONSE: *THE INDEPENDENT*

Carnegie's philanthropy was not without controversy. Some recipients of his gifts resented the demands he placed on them, as for example when he required towns to stock books in and maintain the libraries he built for them. A few prominent theologians questioned whether his philosophy of wealth was really Christian, some saying that ill-gotten gain could never result in any good, others that he was only trying to assuage his guilt by giving so much away, still others that giving money to the poor only encouraged them to be dependent. Some laborers questioned the value of money spent on libraries: an elevator operator told a journalist he had never seen a book that cured starvation.

But many people, both in America and in Britain, gave Carnegie unquestioning praise for his philanthropy, and the praise grew with the gifts. These people forgave him for the way his wealth was amassed, and they overlooked the way he dictated how his money was to be spent. They did not resent the fact that his wealth was created by an overworked labor force or that he did not trust the masses to spend his money for the cultural and educational purposes he knew were best for them. They agreed with a journalist who called him, with inaccurate but understandable verbal construction, "the first multimillionaire to feel the prick of social consciousness." Typical of the opinion that Carnegie was a secular saint was the following comment, "The Fine Art of Giving," which appeared in *The Independent,* just after Carnegie's eightieth birthday in 1915, when the full extent of his philanthropy was known.

> To give away $400,000,000 wisely requires more ability and of a rarer kind than to accumulate it. Mr. Carnegie on his eightieth birthday is to be congratulated on having made so few enemies and aroused so little serious criticism. All of the objects which he has endowed—public libraries, professors' pensions, scientific research, industrial education, and promotion of peace—are universally recognized as worthy, and the only fault found with them has come from those who thought he should have something more or something else.

As we pointed out many years ago, Mr. Carnegie is entitled to be called "the greatest socialist in the world." For the fundamental principle of all the various forms of socialism is the transference of private wealth to public purposes. If, then, socialism consists in actually accomplishing this instead of merely talking about it, Mr. Carnegie is a greater socialist than any who bear the name, from Karl Marx and Lasalle to Liebknecht and Jaures. His gifts for library buildings are conditional upon the community providing the site and agreeing to support the library to the amount of at least ten per cent per annum of what he gives, so in the course of time his original donation will be but a small part of what he has induced others to give. It is, then, not $400,000,000 but more than ten times that which he has caused to be transferred from private to public and semi-public uses.

Reformers are apt to consider themselves rather radical if they advocate the imposition of a tax of twenty or fifty per cent on great fortunes. But Mr. Carnegie has gone far beyond their most ambitious schemes in that he has during his lifetime voluntarily contributed ninety-five per cent of his total wealth.

ESTABLISHMENT RESPONSE: ELIHU ROOT

Praise came also from the conservative establishment, from men of wealth and position themselves who saw in his philanthropy both a way to prevent some future socialist government from confiscating their property and a way to make a favorable impression on the exploited public. Such men also saw dangers in Carnegie's example and were careful to raise flags of caution. They lauded Carnegie's largesse but carefully detailed why and how he made his grants. His philanthropy was rational, sensible, as befitted a man of business acumen. It was not required of all, and when given it must be done in a reasonable manner, as Mr. Carnegie made his gifts.

Perhaps the best example of this kind of cautionary admiration was voiced by Elihu Root at the before-mentioned Authors' Club Memorial Dinner in New York in April 1920. Root praised Carnegie's liberal distribution of wealth, but he also took pains to explain the steel merchant's motivations, goals, and precautions.

A great many of the people of the United States and of the world have learned to think of Mr. Carnegie as a man who had amassed a great fortune and had given away large sums of money. That is a very inadequate and a very inaccurate view. He did amass a great fortune and he did in one sense, a very limited sense, give away great sums of money, but he was predominately of the constructive type. . . .

———

. . . He never, in any ordinary sense, gave away his fortune. He used his fortune, and what may seem to some casual observer the giving away was the securing of agents for the use of his fortune to carry out his purposes.

He brought to the work in the second period of his life, this greatest work of his life, some very marked characteristics. First was the urgency to do, to continue to do something.

Another was the distinct understanding of the difference between using his money for the purpose that he had in his own mind and being a mark for others to make an instrument of him for their purposes. He had also a very distinct understanding of the difficulty of making a good use of money. He knew how easy it was to waste it. He knew what a danger there was of doing harm by the use of it, and he applied to the problem of its use the same sagacity that he applied to the problem of making steel and marketing it.

———

. . . [H]e never held the grab-bag, and he brought to the consideration of the way in which he should use his money not only great sagacity but great pains and assiduity and continuous labor.

Another thing which played a great part in this second period of his life was that he had a very definite conception as to what would contribute to human happiness. In that conception, the mere possession of money played no part. It did not enter his mind that he could in general make men happy by giving them money; but he had brought from his boyhood memories of the longings of the little Scotch weaver's boy. From close, intimate contact with the poor, from the daily round of dreary toil, he had brought a knowledge of the human heart, such as Lincoln brought to the problems of our country during the stress of the Civil War from his experience as a boy.

Doubtless, as he watched the stationary engine which was his task in Pittsburgh, as he stood at the machine of the telegrapher, as he went to his daily duties as Division Superintendent of the Pennsylvania Railroad, he had had his dreams. He had built his palaces in the clouds, and from the heart of the boy, that never left him, he translated his longings into his theory of the possibilities of human happiness.

He said something in his letter to the trustees in establishing the Dunfermline Trust which told the story. He said to them that it gave great pleasure "to bring into the monotonous lives of the toiling masses of Dunfermline more of sweetness and light."

Then there is the last characteristic that I shall mention. He was the kindliest man I ever knew. Wealth had brought to him no hardening of the heart, nor made him forget the dreams of youth. Kindly, affectionate, charitable in his judgments, unrestrained in his sympathy, noble in his impulses, I wish all the people who think of his as a rich man giving away money he did not need could know of the hundreds of kindly things that he did unknown to the world—the old friends remembered, the widows and children cared for, the tender memories of his youth, and all who were associated with him.

And so with this great constructive energy, with this discriminating Scotch sagacity, with this accurate conception of the possibilities of the use of money, with these definite views as to the sources of human happiness, and with this heart overflowing with kindness, he entered upon his second career, undertaking to use these hundreds of millions and not to waste them.

The first thing that he did was to turn to the associates of his early struggles and his early successes. He had done many charitable things, as men ordinarily do, while still engaged in business. But when he came to the dividing line between money-getting and the money-using epochs, he turned to Pittsburgh. And he first attempted there to apply his theories to the possibilities of giving happiness. He began with a library, the endowment of a great library, and he tells us what it was that led him to that.

It was the memory of a library of four hundred volumes which Colonel Anderson of Allegheny, over across the river from Pittsburgh, had opened for the use of the boys when Andrew Carnegie was too poor to buy a book. The first thing he did was to use his money to swing open for others the door of knowledge which gave to him the bright light, the little learning, that could come from Colonel Anderson's four hundred volumes.

He endowed a great library. And then he established the Institute of Pittsburgh. That was the first great reaction of this hard-headed steel-maker—the establishment of the Institute of Pittsburgh in which he invested nearly $30,000,000. Under it he established an art museum and a music hall and a museum of science. For he knew by the knowledge that came from the experience of his life that after men and women have all that is necessary to eat and to wear and for shelter, come great opportunities for increase of happiness in cultivation of taste, in the cultivation of appreciation for the beautiful in the world.

[In his home town of Dunfermline he created] a great park in which he set gardens, play-grounds and gymnasiums and swimming baths, and a sanitary school and a library, in order that recreation and joyful things might come to lighten up the days of toil.

Then he made his gift to the four universities of Scotland—St. Andrews, Glasgow, Aberdeen, and Edinburgh. Ten million dollars he

Cartoon of Carnegie the advocate of negotiation as a winged "Angel of Peace."

gave to them—these universities, toward which he had never been able to bend his steps in youth—one half to be used for improving the university and developing the teaching of science, history, economics, and modern language, and one half to pay the fees of the young men of Scotland who were unable to pay for themselves, giving to all the Scotch boys the opportunity that had been denied to him.

. . . broadening his view, he turned his attention to the maintenance of peace, and with an impulse so natural to establish a hero fund for encouraging and noting properly the heroism of those who lived in peace and in competition with the popular worship of heroism in war. . . . And he moved one step further and established the Endowment for Interntional Peace. . . .

He built the great Peace Palace at The Hague, to strike the imagination of the world with the idea of peace rather than war. He built the Pan-American building at Washington, to furnish a centre for good understanding and friendly intercourse between North and South America. He built a great building for the Central American Court of Justice in Costa Rica. He established another trust for the special use of the churches in their work in favor of peace.

I said that he had not been giving away his money in the strict sense. Far from it. He secured as the agents for the use of his money, for the accomplishment of his noble and beneficent purposes, a great body of men whom no salaries could have attracted, whom no payment could have induced to serve; but who served because the inherent value of the purposes to which Mr. Carnegie summoned them commanded them to serve. . . .

The world has not been able yet to appreciate Mr. Carnegie. We who knew him and loved him and honored him can now express our judgment, but we are about to pass away. Yet the works that he inaugurated are upon so great a scale and are designed to accomplish such great purposes that as the years, the generations, and the centuries go on, they will the more clearly exhibit the true character of the founder. Centuries later men of science will be adding to human knowledge, teachers will be opening the book of learning to the young, friends of peace will be winning the children of civilization from brutality to kindliness; and Andrew Carnegie, the little Scotch weaver's son, will live in the evermore manifest greatness of the achievement that was the outcome of his great and noble heart.

LITERARY RESPONSE:
EDWARD BELLAMY'S *LOOKING BACKWARD*

Writing his novel *Looking Backward* in the mid-1880s, as Carnegie amassed his fortune and began considering a philosophical rationale that would explain why he wanted to give it away, Edward Bellamy foresaw a solution to the unequal distribution of wealth very different from that of Carnegie's "gospel." As Julian West smoked cigars with his host Dr. Leete, he learned what had happened to America in the twentieth century, which of course was Bellamy's plan for the future.

Bellamy's "utopia" did not come through the philanthropy of rich men. It came through consolidations and monopolies.

In the United States there was not, after the beginning of the last quarter of the century, any opportunity whatever for individual enterprise in any important field of industry, unless backed by great capital. During the last decade of the century, such small businesses as still remained were fast-failing survivals of a past epoch, or mere parasites on the great corporations, or else existed in fields too small to attract the great capitalists. Small businesses, as far as they still remained, were reduced to the condition of rats and mice, living in holes and corners, and counting on evading notice for the enjoyment of existence. The railroads had gone on combining till a few great syndicates controlled every rail in the land. In manufactories, every important staple was controlled by a syndicate. These syndicates, pools, trusts, or whatever their name, fixed prices and crushed all competition except when combinations as vast as themselves arose. Then a struggle, resulting in a still greater consolidation, ensued. The great city bazar crushed its country rivals with branch stores, and in the city itself absorbed its smaller rivals till the business of a whole quarter was concentrated under one roof, with a hundred former proprietors of shops serving as clerks. Having no business of his own to put his money in, the small capitalist, at the same time that he took service under the corporation, found no other investment for his money but its stocks and bonds, thus becoming doubly dependent upon it.

The fact that the desperate popular opposition to the consolidation of business in a few powerful hands had no effect to check it proves that there must have been a strong economical reason for it. The small capitalists, with their innumerable petty concerns, had in fact yielded the field to the great aggregations of capital, because they belonged to a day of small things and were totally incompetent to the demands of an age of steam and telegraphs and the gigantic scale of its enterprises. To restore the former order of things, even if possible, would have involved returning to the day of stage-coaches. Oppressive and intolerable as was the regime of the great consolidations of capital, even its victims, while they cursed it, were forced to admit the prodigious increase of efficiency which had been imparted to the national industries, the vast economies effected by concentration of management and unity of organization, and to confess that since the new system had taken the place of the old the wealth of the world had increased at a rate before undreamed of. To be sure this vast increase had gone chiefly to make the rich richer, increasing the gap between them and the poor; but the fact remained that, as a means merely of producing wealth, capital had been proved efficient in proportion to its consolidation. The restoration of the old system with the subdivision of capital, if it were possible, might indeed bring back a greater equality of conditions, with more individual dignity and freedom, but it would be at the price of general poverty and the arrest of material progress.

———

. . . The movement toward the conduct of business by larger and larger aggregations of capital, the tendency toward monopolies, which had been so desperately and vainly resisted, was recognized at last, in its true significance, as a process which only needed to complete its logical evolution to open a golden future to humanity.

Early in the last century the evolution was completed by the final consolidation of the entire capital of the nation. The industry and commerce of the country, ceasing to be conducted by a set of irresponsible corporations and syndicates of private persons at their caprice and for their profit, were intrusted to a single syndicate representing the people, to be conducted in the common interest for the common profit. The nation, that is to say, organized as the one great business corporation in which all other corporations were absorbed; it became the one capitalist in the place of all other capitalists, the sole employer, the final monopoly in which all previous and lesser monopolies were swallowed up, a monopoly in profits and economies of which all citizens shared. The epoch of trusts had ended in The Great Trust. In a word, the people of the United States concluded to assume the conduct of their own business, just as one hundred odd years before they had assumed the conduct of their own government, organizing now for industrial purposes on precisely the same grounds that they had then organized for political purposes.

———

. . . There was absolutely no violence. The change had been long forseen. Public opinion had become fully ripe for it, and the whole mass of the people was behind it. There was no more possibility of opposing it by force than by argument. On the other hand the popular sentiment toward the great corporations and those identified with them had ceased to be one of bitterness, as they came to realize their necessity as a link, a transitional phase, in the evolution of the true industrial system. . . .

PROGRESSIVE RESPONSE: POLITICAL AND ECONOMIC REFORM

Looking Backward was Edward Bellamy's dream of how robber baron America might evolve into industrial unity, owned and operated by the people for the people. Bellamy believed that the country was on the right course, just at an awkward stage in its development, and that equality and justice for the workingman were just a matter of traveling some distance up the road. He saw no future in having individual industrialists like Carnegie amass and distribute personal fortunes. The answer was total consolidation, followed by public ownership. Bellamy was a minority voice, however, in the cacophony of analyses and proposals that rose at the height of industrial capitalism.

Populists and Progressives had a quicker remedy: the federal government should curb the power of wealthy individuals so that the great majority of citizens might share in the wealth being produced. Their themes were adopted by politicians in both major parties, and during the period from 1904 to 1914 both Progressive Republicans and Democrats made modest attempts to level the playing field of American economics.

In 1912 former President Theodore Roosevelt, after a four year "holiday" from politics, sought the Republican nomination in order to return to the White House. During the time he had been out of office he had grown even more Progressive than he had been when president; and he was displeased with the lack of progress made by his hand-picked successor William Howard Taft. When the Republicans played it safe and renominated Taft, Roosevelt formed a new Progressive Party, popularly known as the Bull Moose Party because when accepting its nomination he claimed to be as strong as a bull moose.

Although he lost in November, splitting the Republican vote and helping elect president another Progressive, Democrat Woodrow Wilson, he and his party left a permanent mark on American politics. The following excerpts from Roosevelt's Progressive Party Platform of 1912 offer solutions to industrial injustice and inequality and identify the federal government as the necessary catalyst for change, for progress.

> This country belongs to the people who inhabit it. Its resources, its business, its institutions and its laws should be utilized, maintained or altered in whatever manner will best promote the general interest.
>
> ———
>
> The supreme duty of the Nation is the conservation of human resources through an enlightened measure of social and industrial justice. We pledge ourselves to work unceasingly in State and Nation for:—
> Effective legislation looking to the prevention of industrial accidents, occupational diseases, overwork, involuntary unemployment, and other injurious effects incident to modern industry;

The fixing of minimum safety and health standards for the various occupations, and the exercise of the public authority of State and Nation, including the Federal control over inter-State commerce and the taxing power, to maintain such standards;

The prohibition of child labor;

Minimum wage standards for working women, to provide a living scale in all industrial occupations;

The prohibition of night work for women and the establishment of an eight hour day for women and young persons;

One day's rest in seven for all wage-workers;

The abolition of the convict contract labor system; substituting a system of prison production for governmental consumption only; and the application of prisoners' earnings to the support of their dependent families;

Publicity as to wages, hours and conditions and labor; full reports upon industrial accidents and diseases, and the opening to public inspection of all tallies, weights, measures and check systems on labor products;

Standards of compensation for death by industrial accident and injury and trade diseases which will transfer the burden of lost earnings from the families of working people to the industry, and thus to the community;

The protection of home life against the hazards of sickness, irregular employment and old age through the adoption of a system of social insurance adapted to American use;

The development of the creative labor power of America by lifting the last load of illiteracy from American youth and establishing continuation schools for industrial education under public control and encouraging agricultural education and demonstration in rural schools;

The establishment of industrial research laboratories to put the methods and discoveries of science at the service of American producers;

We favor the organization of the workers, men and women, as a means of protecting their interests and of promoting their progress.

———

We believe that the true popular government, justice and prosperity go hand in hand, and so believing, it is our purpose to secure that large measure of general prosperity which is the fruit of legitimate and honest business, fostered by equal justice and by sound progressive laws.

We demand that the test of true prosperity shall be the benefits conferred thereby on all the citizens not confined to individuals or classes and that the test of corporate efficiency shall be the ability better to serve the public; that those who profit by control of business affairs shall justify that profit and that control by sharing with the public the fruits thereof.

SOCIALIST RESPONSE: EUGENE V. DEBS'S REVOLUTION

Progressivism influenced American politics for decades. It was responsible for most of the economic reforms before the New Deal. Still, the Progressives were moderates compared to early twentieth-century Socialists, who called for radical governmental action to right the wrongs done to American workers by the robber barons. Their most eloquent spokesman was labor leader and repeated candidate for president Eugene V. Debs.

Debs did not think the Progressives went far enough in their proposed reforms, and he completely rejected Carnegie's philosophy of philanthropy. He condemned Carnegie for using violence against his workingmen at Homestead and for accumulating an immense fortune at the expense of the men's labor. Homestead, along with other broken strikes of the 1890s, convinced him that capitalists could not be trusted, even when they offered to make public grants under the guise of a gospel of wealth. A man who would use an army of thugs to break a strike, when all the strikers wanted was a living wage, could not in old age compensate for his sins by turning himself into a philanthropist.

> Carnegie, to use a phrase, "gets religion," and begins to blubber about the duty of rich men to the poor. He out-phariseed all the pharisees who made broad their phylacteries and made long prayers on the corners of the streets in Jerusalem that they might be seen of men, while they were "devouring widows' houses" and binding burdens on the backs of men grievous to be borne, for Carnegie, bent on show and parade, seeking applause, ambitious of notoriety, concluded to bestow a portion of his plunder to build libraries bearing his name to perpetuate his fame.
>
> This Andrew Carnegie, in 1889, began to preach his "Gospel of Wealth," the purpose of which was to demonstrate that wealth creates "rigid castes," not unlike those that exist in India among the followers of the Brahmin religion the Carnegies being the priests and the workingmen the pariahs, and this Brahminism of wealth being established, Carnegie, the author of the "gospel," lays back on his couch of down and silk and writes, this condition "is best for the race because it insures the survival of the fittest."

Under the influence of his "Gospel of Wealth," Carnegie, having prospered prodigiously, having millions at his command, concluded that the time had arrived for him to array himself in purple and parade before the people of Great Britain. He was ambitious of applause. He wanted to sit in an open carriage drawn by a half dozen spanking high steppers and hear the roar of the groundlings as the procession moved along the streets. In the United States Carnegie was not held in much higher esteem than Robert Kidd. . . .

Indeed, the freebooter never robbed as many men as Andrew Carnegie, though their methods were somewhat different. Kidd never wrote a "Gospel of Wealth." He never played the role of hypocrite. When he struck a rich prize on the high seas, captured the valuables, killed the crew and sunk the ship, he did not go ashore and bestow his booty to build a church or found a library; but, like Carnegie, he was influenced by a "Gospel of Wealth," which was to get all he could and live luxuriously while he lived and then, like the rich man spoken of in the New Testament, go to "hell."

Debs concluded that Carnegie was no more than a brazen pirate, a "Christless capitalist" who plundered labor in order to erect his churches, endow his universities, and build his libraries. His "good works" were bought with blood; and his plutocratic, pharisaic philanthropy was hollow. Debs educated himself by reading American (Bellamy) and European (Marx) social theorists; and he eventually rejected not only capitalism but the policies of labor leaders such as Samuel Gompers who supported the capitalist system so long as workers got a piece of the pie. Debs concluded that only Socialism, under which workers were guaranteed the wealth they produced, would give equality and justice. Through socialism the workers would "break their fetters and rise to the dignity of free men." Socialism would "abolish the capitalist political state and clear the way for industrial and social democracy." Socialism would be achieved not just through the vote but by organization and industrial action. "Get ready, comrades, for action!" Debs wrote in the March 10, 1906 issue of the Socialist paper *Appeal to Reason*, "No other course is left to the working class."

RELIGIOUS RESPONSE:
WALTER RAUSCHENBUSCH'S SOCIAL GOSPEL

Both Carnegie in his philanthropic musings and Debs in his oratorical flourishes used a distinctly and overtly Christian vocabulary, each to buttress his opinions with language that had power over American audiences. The same was true of two other outspoken social activists of the day, Jane Addams and Walter Rauschenbusch. Addams and Rauschenbush, like Debs, were suspicious of Carnegie's philanthropy and offered   alternatives. Each one advocated a form of Christian socialism.

Addams was the founder of Hull House in Chicago, where young women were trained for life in the inner city. She and her fellow advocates of "Settlement" houses believed both that social work was the essence of Christianity and that the contributor of funds must share the life of the people he is trying to help. In an address given in 1892 Addams said, "The impulse to share the lives of the poor, the desire to make social service, irrespective of propaganda, express the spirit of Christ, is as old as Christianity itself." The earliest Christians, she said, ". . . longed to share the common lot that they might receive the common revelation." They sought ". . . The joy of finding the Christ which lieth in each man, but which no man can unfold save in fellowship." Philanthropic giving was good and even necessary to the success of social work, but Addams found Carnegie's form of philanthropy, granting money without sharing the lives of the recipients, woefully inadequate.

Walter Rauschenbusch's thoughts about philanthropy were formed when as a young pastor in the rough Hell's Kitchen section of New York City he saw how inadequate traditional religious thinking was to address the needs of modern urban society. When in later years he became a professor of theology and had the time to put his ideas into books, he became the most articulate spokesman for what came to be known as the "Social Gospel." This gospel taught that saving souls was only one part of the Christian's responsibility to his fellow man; just as important was the duty to save bodies and minds. The following excerpts from his book *Christianizing the Social Order* outlined Rauschenbusch's plan of Christian socialism, which he believed was the plan envisioned by Jesus and the early Christians. In the first, although he did not call him by name, he obviously had Carnegie in mind. In order to fulfill Christ's plan of sharing, the philanthropist must admit that his wealth came from sinful enterprises. He must repent his capitalistic theft of his fellow man's labor. He must do what he can to assure that no one in the future makes such wealth at the expense of his fellow man.

> Every rich man who has taken the Christian doctrine of stewardship
> seriously has thereby expropriated himself after a fashion and
> become manager where he used to be owner. If a man in addition
> realizes that some part of his fortune consists of unearned money,
> accumulated by one of the forms of injustice which have been

legalized by our social order, it becomes his business as a Christian and a gentleman to make restitution in some way. There is no sincere repentance without restitution and confession of wrong. If I discovered that I or my grandfather had, knowingly or unknowingly, by some manipulation or error of the survey, added to my farm a ten-acre strip which belonged to my neighbor, could I go on harvesting the crops on it and say nothing? It is true that restitution of wealth absorbed from great communities through many years is a complicated matter, and that the giving away of large sums is dangerous business which may do as much harm as good. Yet some way must be found. Since the rich have gained their wealth by appropriating public functions and by using the taxing powers which ought to belong to the community alone, the fittest way of restitution is to undertake public service for which the State in its present impoverished condition has no means, such as the erection and running of public baths, playgrounds, and civic centers. But the moral value of such gifts would be almost incalculably increased if some acknowledgment were made that these funds were drawn from the people and belonged to them. Every time any rich man has indicated that he felt troubled in mind about his right to his wealth, the public heart has warmed toward him with a sense of forgiveness. If some eminent man should have the grace and wisdom to make a confession of wrong on behalf of his whole class, it would have a profound influence on public morality and social peace.

If a rich man has a really redeemed conscience and intellect, the best way to give away his unearned wealth would be to keep it and use it as a tool to make the recurrence of such fortunes as his own forever impossible. The Salvation Army sets a saved girl to save other girls, and that is the best way to keep her saved. By the same token a man whose forefathers made their money in breweries or distilleries ought to use it to fight alcoholism; a man who made his by land speculation should help to solve the housing question or finance the single-tax movement; a man who has charged monopoly prices for the necessities of life should teach the people to organize cooperative societies. . . .

These words were mild by Rauschenbusch's standards. In much of his writing he thundered with prophetic zeal. The way Carnegie and his fellow industrialists earned their wealth was itself an evil enterprise. He shocked conservative theologians of his day, the kind who admired and praised Carnegie for his philanthropy, by declaring bluntly that Christianity and capitalism were incompatible.

Life is holy. Respect for life is Christian. Business, setting Profit first, has recklessly used up the life of the workers, and impaired the life of the consumers whenever that increased profit. The life of great masses has been kept low by poverty, haunted by fear, and deprived of the joyous expression of life in play.

Beauty is a manifestation of God. Capitalism is ruthless of the beauty of nature if its sacrifice increases profit. When commerce appeals to the sense of beauty in its products, beauty is a device to make profit, and becomes meretricious, untrue, and sometimes corrupts the sense of beauty. Neither does the distribution of wealth under capitalism offer the best incentives to artistic ability.

Love is of God; the home is its sanctuary. Capitalism is breaking down or crippling the home wherever it prevails, and poisoning society with the decaying fragments of what was the spring house of life. The conditions created by capitalism are the conditions in which prostitution is multiplying. Some sections of capitalistic business are directly interested in vice and foster it. Because it is so immensely profitable the white slave traffic would speedily become a great industry if the State did not repress it; and where the State tries to grapple with it, commercialized vice is corrupting the officers of the State.

Devotion to the common good is one of the holy and divine forces in human society.

Capitalism teaches us to set private interest before the common good. It follows profit, and not patriotism and public spirit. If it is necessary to create or protect profit, it will involve nations in war, but it plays a selfish part amid the sacrifices imposed by war. It organizes many of the ablest men into powerful interests which are at some points antagonistic to the interest of the community. It has corrupted our legislatures, our executive officers, and our courts, tampered with the organs of public opinion and instruction, spread a spirit of timidity among the citizens, and vindictively opposed the men who stood for the common good against the private interests.

———

Religion declares the supreme value of life and personality, even the humblest; Business negatives that declaration of faith by setting up Profit as the supreme and engrossing object of thought and effort, and by sacrificing life to profit where necessary.

Christianity teaches the unity and solidarity of men; Capitalism reduces that teaching to a harmless expression of sentiment by splitting society into two antagonistic sections, unlike in their work, their income, their pleasures, and their point of view.

True Christianity wakens men to a sense of their worth, to love of freedom, and independence of action; Capitalism, based on the principle of autocracy, resents independence, suppresses the attempts of the working class to gain it, and deadens the awakening effect that goes out from Christianity. The spirit of Christianity puts even men of unequal worth on a footing of equality by the knowledge of common sin and weakness, and by the faith in a common salvation; Capitalism creates an immense inequality between families, perpetuates it by property conditions, and makes it hard for high and low to have a realizing sense of the equality which their religion teaches.

Christianity puts the obligation of love on the holiest basis and exerts its efforts to create fraternal feeling among men, and to restore it where broken; Capitalism has created world-wide unrest, jealousy, resentment, and bitterness, which choke Christian love with weeds.

Jesus bids us strive first for the Reign of God and the justice of God, because on that spiritual basis all material wants too will be met; Capitalism urges us to strive first and last for our personal enrichment, and it formerly held out the hope that the selfishness of all would create the universal good.

Christianity makes the love of money the root of all evil, and demands the exclusion of the covetous and extortioners from the Christian fellowship; Capitalism cultivates the love of money for its own sake and gives its largest wealth to those who use monopoly for extortion.

Thus two spirits are wrestling for the mastery in modern life, the spirit of Christ and the spirit of Mammon. . . .

The Christian solution to social and economic inequality and therefore to the injustice of the capitalist system, said Rauschenbusch, was not the philanthropy of a Carnegie. He labeled Carnegie's way a "shortcut" to immortality that bypassed confession of wrongdoing and did not really deserve the love and gratitude of men. The Christian solution was the socialization, the public ownership of property.

When the robber barons along the Rhine levied tribute on the merchants teaming along the road, they partly desocialized the great trade route of the river valley. When the burghers of the commercial towns bought them off for a lump sum, they partly resocialized the public highway, and when they finally rased the barons' castles as nests of social vermin, they socialized the road more fully. When the Interstate Commerce Commission in 1912 compelled the Express Companies to improve their antiquated service and to lower their extortionate charges, it partly socialized a great branch of transportation, and when Congress at last established the parcels post, it socialized the same branch more fully.

By "socializing property" we mean, then, that it is made to serve the public good, either by the service its uses render to the public welfare, or by the income it brings to the public treasury. In point of fact, however, no important form of property can be entirely withdrawn from public service; human life is too social in its nature to allow it. If a rich man builds a ten-foot wall around his estate and admits nobody, the birds will still nest and sing there to the poorest passer-by, and his trees will produce oxygen that is wafted to the slum. Socializing property will mean, therefore, that instead of serving the welfare of a small group directly, and the public welfare only indirectly, it will be made more directly available for the service of all.

ASSESSMENTS OF CARNEGIE'S PHILANTHROPY BY ROBERT HEILBRONER AND JUDITH SEALANDER

Economist Robert Heilbroner and historian Judith Sealander have explored the motivations for and effectiveness of Carnegie's philanthropy. In his "Epitaph for the Steel Master," Heilbroner discussed how from the earliest period of his career Carnegie's deepest desires were in conflict with his drive to make money.

It was certainly as "the richest man in the world" that Carnegie attracted the attention of his contemporaries. Yet this is hardly why we look back on him with interest today. As an enormous money-maker Carnegie was a flashy, but hardly a profound, hero of the times; and the attitudes of Earnestness and Self-Assurance, so engaging in the young immigrant, become irritating when they are congealed in the millionaire. But what lifts Carnegie's life above the rut of a one-dimensional success story is an aspect of which his contemporaries were relatively unaware.

Going through his papers after his death, Carnegie's executors came across a memorandum that he had written to himself fifty years before, carefully preserved in a little yellow box of keepsakes and mementos. It brings us back to December, 1868, when Carnegie, a young man flushed with the first taste of great success, retired to his suite in the opulent Hotel St. Nicholas in New York, to tot up his profits for the year. It had been a tremendous year and the calculation must have been extremely pleasurable. Yet this is what he wrote as he reflected on the future:

Thirty-three and an income of $50,000 per annum! By this time two years I can so arrange all my business as to secure at least $50,000 per annum. Beyond this never earn—make no effort to increase fortune, but spend the surplus each year for benevolent purposes. Cast aside business forever, except for others. Settle in Oxford and get a thorough education, making the acquaintance of literary men—this will take three years of active work—pay especial attention to speaking in public. Settle then in London and purchase a controlling interest in some newspaper or live review and give the general management of it attention, taking part in public matters, especially those connected with education and improvement of the poorer classes.

Man must have an idol—the amassing of wealth is one of the worst species of idolatry—no idol more debasing than the worship of money. Whatever I engage in I must push inordinately; therefore should I be careful to choose that life which will be the most elevating in its character. To continue much longer overwhelmed by business cares and with most of my thoughts wholly upon the way to make more money in the shortest time, must degrade me beyond hope of permanent recovery. I will resign business at thirty-five, but during the ensuing two years I wish to spend the afternoons in receiving instruction and in reading systematically.

It is a document which in more ways than one is Carnegie to the very life: brash, incredibly self-confident, chockablock with self-conscience virtue—and more than a little hypocritical. For the program so nobly outlined went largely unrealized. Instead of retiring in two years, Carnegie went on for thirty-three more; even then it was with considerable difficulty that he was persuaded to quit. Far from shunning further money-making, he proceeded to roll up his fortune with an uninhibited drive that led one unfriendly biographer to characterize him as "the greediest little gentleman ever created." Certainly he was one of the most aggressive profit seekers of his time. Typically, when an associate jubilantly cabled: "No. 8 furnace broke all records today," Carnegie coldly replied, "What were the other furnaces doing?"

It is this contrast between his hopes and his performance that makes Carnegie interesting.

For when we review his life, what we see is more than the career of another nineteenth-century acquisitor. We see the unequal struggle between a man who loved money—loved making it, having it, spending it—and a man who, at bottom, was ashamed of himself for his acquisitive desires. All during his lifetime, the money-maker seemed to win. But what lifts Carnegie's story out of the ordinary is that the other Carnegie ultimately triumphed. At his death public speculation placed the size of his estate at about five hundred million dollars. In fact it came to $22,881,575. Carnegie *had* become the richest man in the world—but something had also driven him to give away ninety per cent of his wealth.

Heilbroner then discussed Carnegie's gospel of wealth and how he had shocked many of his contemporaries by his argument that the millionaire should give away his fortune.

Coming from the leading millionaire of the day, these had been startling sentiments. So also were his views on the "labor question"
which, if patronizing, were nonetheless humane and advanced for
their day. The trouble was, of course that the sentiments were somewhat difficult to credit. As one commentator of the day remarked,
"His vision of what might be done with wealth had beauty and
breadth and thus serenely overlooked the means by which wealth
had been acquired."

Meanwhile there had also come fame and honors in which
Carnegie wallowed unashamedly. He counted the "freedoms"
bestowed on him by grateful or hopeful cities and crowed, "I have
fifty-two and Gladstone has only seventeen." He entertained the
King of England and told him that democracy was better than
monarchy, and met the German Kaiser: "Oh yes, yes," said the latter
worthy on being introduced. "I have read your books. You do not
like kings." But Mark Twain, on hearing of this, was not fooled. "He
says he is a scorner of kings and emperors and dukes," he wrote,
"whereas he is like the rest of the human race: a slight attention
from one of these can make him drunk for a week. . . ."

And yet it is not enough to conclude that Carnegie was in fact a
smaller man than he conceived himself. For this judgment over-
looks one immense and irrefutable fact. He did, in the end, abide
by his self-imposed duty. He did give nearly all of his gigantic fortune away.

As one would suspect, the quality of the philanthropy reflected
the man himself. There was, for example, a huge and sentimentally
administered private pension fund to which access was to be had
on the most trivial as well as the most worthy grounds: if it included a number of writers, statesmen, scientists, it also made room for
two maiden ladies with whom Carnegie had once danced as a
young man, a boyhood acquaintance who had once held Carnegie's
books while he ran a race, a merchant to whom he had once delivered a telegram and who had subsequently fallen on hard times. And
then, as one would expect, there was a benevolent autocracy in the
administration of the larger philanthropies as well. "Now everybody
vote Aye," was the way Carnegie typically determined the policies of
the philanthropic "foundations" he established.

Yet if these flaws bore the stamp of one side of Carnegie's personality, there was also the other side—the side that, however
crudely, asked important questions and however piously, concerned
itself with great ideals. Of this the range and purpose of the main
philanthropies gave unimpeachable testimony. . . . In his instructions to the trustees of [the Carnegie Foundation], couched in the
simplified spelling of which he was an ardent advocate, we see
Carnegie at his very best:

Conditions on erth inevitably change; hence, no wise man will bind Trustees forever to certain paths, causes, or institutions. I disclaim my intention of doing so. . . . My chief happiness, as I write these lines in the thot that, even after I pass away, the welth that came to me to administer as a sacred trust for the good of my fellow men is to continue to benefit humanity. . . .

If these sentiments move us—if Carnegie himself in retrospect moves us at last to grudging respect—it is not because his was the triumph of a saint or a philosopher. It is because it was the much more difficult triumph of a very human and fallible man struggling to retain his convictions in an age, and in the face of a career, which subjected them to impossible temptations. Carnegie is something of America writ large; his is the story of the Horatio Alger hero *after* he has made his million dollars. In the failures of Andrew Carnegie we see many of the failures of America itself. In his curious triumph, we see what we hope is our own steadfast core of integrity.

Judith Sealander's book *Private Wealth and Public Life* is a study of the many foundations established during the past century by wealthy American individuals and families; and it offers an interesting alternative interpretation of Carnegie's philanthropy. She concluded from her research into the world of public giving that Carnegie's *Gospel of Wealth* philosophy and the various foundations he established were not as great an influence on "scientific giving" as many people think. She said that "the other philanthropists . . . rarely consulted Andrew Carnegie. Occasionally, but always in secret, they mocked him."

For one thing, Carnegie advised donors to give all their wealth away within their own lifetimes. Indeed, in his opinion, those among the very wealthy who chose to let their relatives inherit great riches thwarted the rise of the most fit to leadership. Each generation should create its own great fortunes from scratch for a true meritocracy to exist. This was a view that Carnegie's fellow philanthropists, even if they worried about the bad influence of inherited wealth, did not support. . . . Not a single other major philanthropist of the early twentieth century followed Carnegie's advice that wealth was a "curse," and that heirs should receive nothing.

Second, Carnegie's "Wealth" espoused an extreme version of Social Darwinism, a version out of keeping with the religious beliefs of most of his peers. The millionaire, the product of a fierce struggle for domination, was society's fittest. He owed his success to himself, or at least to his genes, not to God. This latter idea would have struck most of Carnegie's fellow philanthropists as skirting the edge of blasphemy. They at least paid lip service to divine benevolence as the source of their good fortune.

Finally, the advice given in "Wealth" was not particularly new. In fact, Carnegie's idea exemplified traditional distributive charity, rather than "scientific philanthropy."

Sealander found that Carnegie's philanthropy, fashioned by him and carried out by those he appointed, was elitist. Its keyword was the best of everything. It tended to help train the best minds at the "best" schools to bring the best culture to the masses of people, thus liberating them from bad taste in reading, music, drama, recreation, and life in general.

> The lower orders, however, went on living in bad taste and utter drabness. At least, they stayed away from the Carnegie-sponsored associations, lectures, and workshops. There is no evidence that they followed the literary suggestions made by Carnegie experts and no evidence that they saw Rembrandt with new eyes. The people who composed the sparse audiences for these corporation-funded efforts to elevate American culture were members of the same aspiring middle class that supported the Chautauqua movement. If the Carnegie Corporation practiced cultural imperialism, most of the colonials practiced passive rebellion.

Sealander concluded that most twentieth-century philanthropic foundations have followed the Rockefeller and not the Carnegie pattern. Rockefeller's trustees practiced what she called "wholesale" philanthropy, not the "retail" philanthropy of Carnegie. Wholesale philanthropy funded research rather than erecting buildings. Even the Carnegie trustees, after his death, began to move in that direction.

TED TURNER ON GIVING

Since Carnegie's day, in large part because of the example he and others established, many tycoons have in their later years turned to philanthropy. A tax deduction system which permitted donors to give some of their wealth to worthy causes rather than have it taken away by the government made their philanthropic giving both honorable and practical. John D. Rockefeller surpassed Carnegie in the amount he gave to his chosen charities, although not in the percentage of his fortune he gave; and the $500,000,000 he eventually gave away was worth about the same as Carnegie's over $300,000,000 had earlier been. The list of philanthropists has continued to grow through the twentieth century. In our day it is almost expected that the superwealthy should create foundations to distribute a portion of their gains to public needs. Bill Gates, for example, has to date given over $335,000,000 to projects ranging from computers for libraries to the enhancement of the Seattle Symphony Orchestra to children's cancer research to the control of HIV in Africa. He says he plans eventually to give away $24,000,000,000. On the World Wide Web, there are pages featuring prominent philanthropists who offer grants for various projects, journal articles on philanthropy, and even reviews of philanthropic projects.

On September 18, 1997, at a United Nations Association Dinner at Times Square in New York, billionaire broadcasting magnate Ted Turner received a Global Leadership Award for his financial contributions to the international community. He had made a number of large contributions to worthy causes, and his cable network had sponsored and broadcast the Goodwill Games to promote understanding between nations. It was to be a predictably congratulatory ceremony for a rich contributor; but Turner startled the black-tie audience of diplomats and dignitaries by making the following announcement, obviously not from a prepared text. In fact, no text of his announcement exists, and the following transcription is taken from audio clips of his address found on the World Wide Web.

> I'm going to try my dead-level best—with some qualifications—but not as bad as what the United States asks for—not impossible—but to donate a billion dollars to the U.N. causes myself—and announce it tonight. [Gasps of surprise from the audience]
> The plan is to make it a hundred million a year for ten years. [Cheers]
>
> ———
>
> But I notice I got my monthly statement, you know, we're all businessmen and we get our statements—like the U.N. gets theirs—how much they're in arrears—that sort of thing. [Laughter]
> But I got my statement, and it said that on January 1, I was worth 2,200,000,000 and on August 31, I was worth 3,200,000,000. So all I'm giving away with this billion dollars is my nine-month's earnings. It's not even a full year's worth. Who cares? [More laughter and sustained applause]
>
> ———
>
> And we're going to have a committee of this foundation work with a committee of the U.N. To decide how it gets split up. But the

money can only go to the U.N. causes and go into the funds that
make things better for people all over the world. [Thunderous
applause]

Turner's "last nine months' earnings" comment referred to the billion dollars added to his fortune by the shares he received when his
Turner Broadcasting Corporation merged with the Time-Warner media
conglomerate earlier in 1997. The gift would in fact be given in the
form of stock in the new megamedia empire. The amount roughly
equaled the U.N.'s total budget for one year.

The gift put Turner in a select class of major philanthropists, for
while many others had given hundreds of millions to charity, only three
had reached the one billion dollar level: Walter Annenberg, publisher of
the *Philadelphia Inquirer* and TV Guide; Paul Mellon, owner of Gulf
Oil; and George Soros, president of Soros Fund Management. Vartan
Gregorian, president of the Carnegie Foundation, confirmed soon after
Turner's pledge announcement that Turner's is the largest single donation ever made to any cause. He was gracious enough not to mention
that Carnegie's $300,000,000 would today be worth more than five bil-
lion dollars. He also did not mention Rockefeller's equivalent amount.

Talking later that evening with reporters, then giving an exclusive
interview to his CNN employee, the talk show host Larry King, Turner
explained that the gift would come in installments of one hundred million a year for ten years to the United Nations Foundation, since an individual could not contribute directly to the United Nations, and it would
be designated to fund projects approved by the Secretary General.
"This is not going to go for administration," he said. "This is only going
to go for programs, programs like refugees, cleaning up land mines,
peacekeeping, UNICEF for children, for diseases, and we're going to
have a committee that will work with the committee of the U.N. The
money can only go to U.N. causes."

"With our economy, we've got billionaires on every street corner.
I'm one of them," said the man who rode his broadcasting empire to
world class fame and fortune. "A billion dollars is a lot more money
than you can spend intelligently, so why not spend it for the children
dying of preventable diseases?"

Turner told King, "I have learned—the more good that I did, the
more money comes in. You have to learn to give. You're not born as a
giver. You're born selfish." He also vowed to prod other billionaires to
give money to worthy causes. "If you're rich, you can expect a letter or
a call from me."

Pundits noted the change in Turner's outlook on the world over the past twenty years. He once considered the United Nations just a place where Democrats appeased Communists. Then he began meeting regularly with former President Jimmy Carter, like Turner a Georgian, and Carter's dedication to humanitarian causes opened Turner's eyes to the complexities of world affairs. Then he married activist actress Jane Fonda; and it was with Fonda that he first began considering a gift to U.N. programs. He told King that his decision brought tears to Jane's eyes. "I'm proud to be married to you," she told him when he named the amount. Two years later they were divorced.

Having spent his adult life accumulating a fortune, having achieved heroic status among those who admire moguls, Turner followed Carnegie's example and decided to win the admiration of the rest of the public by becoming a great philanthropist, an American saint.

QUESTIONS FOR CRITICAL EXAMINATION

1. How did Carnegie explain why he wanted to give away his fortune? What did he leave unsaid when he wrote his articles on philanthropy? What questions did his comments raise in your mind? Why did he not discuss the possibility that socialists or communists might try to raid the great American fortunes?

2. Carnegie has been accused of paternalism in his philanthropy. What evidence, if any, do you find for this charge in his "Gospel of Wealth" and in the way he carried out his philanthropic enterprises?

3. What are the strong and weak points of Carnegie's theories about the accumulation and distribution of wealth? How would he be received if he delivered a speech on his attitudes to an audience of university students today?

4. Show how Carnegie used Christian language and concepts to illustrate his theories about the uses of wealth. Since he was not strictly speaking a Christian, why did he do this? What do you feel made him apprehensive about dying rich?

5. What does *The Independent*'s commentary on Carnegie's philanthropy tell you about the popular image of Carnegie after his retirement? What questions about his philanthropy had apparently been raised, and how did the author dispose of them? How did his comments underline the "saintly" image of Carnegie?

6. What emphasis did Elihu Root put on Carnegie's philanthropic endeavors? Why did he feel it necessary to remind audiences of the practical nature of Carnegie's giving?

7. Describe Edward Bellamy's vision of America's industrial future. How did he think America would achieve economic justice and social equality? How do you imagine a conversation between Bellamy and Karl Marx would go? Is Bellamy's vision socialism, communism, or true democracy?

8. In what ways were the Progressive Party's Platform proposals aimed at correcting social and economic problems caused by the age of big industry? Show how their proposals were "moderate," somewhere between *laissez-faire* capitalism and the socialism advocated by Debs and Rauschenbusch?

9. Why did Debs consider Carnegie's philanthropy a sham? What validity did his call for a Socialist revolution have for the America of his day? Why does Debs still today attract some people and repel others?

10. What did Jane Addams and Walter Rauschenbusch say was missing in Carnegie's philanthropy? What would Carnegie have had to do to please each one? What did each one see as the real fulfillment of the Christian gospel?

11. What personal conflicts did Heilbroner say Carnegie wrestled with through his career as a financier? How did he resolve them? Was the Carnegie solution good for the American industrial system and its working class? Explain.

12. What does the Turner announcement tell you about Ted Turner himself and the world in which his gift is being made? In what ways is his philanthropy like and in what ways unlike that of Andrew Carnegie?

Chapter Six

SUGGESTED TOPICS
FOR RESEARCH PAPERS

1. THE FABULOUSLY RICH INDUSTRIALISTS
AND THE AMERICAN DREAM

This paper could analyze the conditions that made possible the rise of America's nineteenth-century industrial barons. It could also describe the effect these men and their achievements had on the American way of thinking down to our own day. Carnegie, Rockefeller, and Ford could be examples.

2. ANDREW CARNEGIE: THE MAN AND HIS WEALTH

This paper could analyze Carnegie's story, as told both by himself and by others, for clues as to how and why he was able to become at one point the world's richest man. It could consider his natural, personal gifts, his Scottish heritage, and the opportunities not available in Britain that America gave him to succeed.

3. THE RAGS TO RICHES MYTH
IN AMERICAN HISTORY AND THOUGHT

This paper could trace the development of the American dream of riches from the early nineteenth century to the present. It could show the part played in its development by men like Carnegie. It could assess how valid it was (and is) for a society in which only a few people have reached the goal of great wealth.

4. THE EMPIRE OF STEEL: CARNEGIE'S BIG BUSINESS

This paper could analyze the way Carnegie built and ran his empire. It could show his production and vending methods and his labor policies. It could consider the American economic and social system of his day and how he learned to use it to his advantage. It could also compare the Carnegie Empire with economic empires today in their development and management.

5. CARNEGIE AND THE ART OF PHILANTHROPY

This paper could analyze Carnegie's motivations for and methods of distributing his wealth through philanthropic endeavors. It could study his successes and failures in this enterprise. It could compare his efforts to those of other men of his age and those who are involved in philanthropy today.

6. ANDREW CARNEGIE'S PLACE IN AMERICAN HISTORY

This paper, broader and more speculative than the others, could assess Carnegie's contributions to American history, how he is viewed by historians today, and how he might be viewed in years to come. Areas of investigation here could be the role of the immigrant in America's development, the conditions and talents needed to win great wealth, the effect Carnegie had on American business, and the influence Carnegie's philanthropy had on other American entrepreneurs.

7. ANDREW CARNEGIE: CREATOR OF THE AMERICAN MIND?

This paper, using Carnegie as the subject, could examine the philosophical question of whether there is in fact an American mind. If you conclude that there is no American mind, how do we best describe the effect Carnegie and people like him had on American history? If you conclude that there is one, what contributions to it did Carnegie and people like him make?

Chapter Seven

ANNOTATED BIBLIOGRAPHY FOR USE IN RESEARCH PAPERS

Horatio Alger. *Risen from the Ranks.* Chicago: Donohue, 1870; and *Ragged Dick.* Philadelphia: John C. Winston, 1910. These are perhaps the most representative of Alger's many novels, all of which portrayed the poor boy who through honest hard work became a successful American businessman. Many of Alger's books have been reprinted by Media Press, and a selected set was published by the *Reprint Services Corporation* of Temecula, California, in 1989. Information is also available at the Web site of the Horatio Alger Society (http://www.ihot.com/~has/).

Bruce Barton. *The Man Nobody Knows.* Indianapolis: Bobbs-Merrill Company, 1925. Barton's book challenged the traditional image of Jesus as a peasant reformer and social critic who suffered without protest for the sins of the world. Barton's Jesus was the first modern businessman who knew how to pick effective assistants, invented the art of advertising, and founded the most successful "corporation" in world history, the Christian Church.

Edward Bellamy. *Looking Backward.* New York: Gosset and Dunlap, 1887. Actually looking forward from 1887 to the year 2000, Bellamy's fantasy about a man who woke up in the future was a critique of late nineteenth-century industrial America. By the year 2000, Americans had abandoned industrial strife and competition; the nation was one big business. Critics have argued whether Bellamy was predicting a future or calling for a return to the morality and economy of an earlier day.

Dwight Burlingame, ed. *Responsibilities of Wealth*. Bloomington: University of Indiana Press, 1994. This volume opens with Carnegie's "Gospel of Wealth," identified as the first comprehensive statement on philanthropy, then provides six other essays on the subject. The authors explore the philosophical and practical bases for public giving and investigate the repercussions as well. Especially intriguing is Louise Knight's essay comparing Carnegie's philosophy of giving to that of Jane Addams, who believed true philanthropy required an encounter between giver and recipient.

Andrew Carnegie. *Autobiography of Andrew Carnegie*. Boston: Houghton-Mifflin, 1924. Published after his death, these memoirs, written in his old age, show Carnegie as he wanted to be remembered. Each chapter covered an episode in his life and career; and the last several described his conversations and correspondence with the intellectuals of his day, among whom he felt he belonged.

Andrew Carnegie. *The Empire of Business*. New York: Greenwood, 1933. This volume contains Carnegie's major speeches and magazine and newspaper articles in which he expounded some of his most important social and economic theories. The most interesting are his "A B C of Money," "How to Win Fortune," and "The Three-Legged Stool."

Andrew Carnegie. *The Gospel of Wealth and Other Essays*. Cambridge: Harvard University Press, 1962. The opening essay is Carnegie's most famous statement about wealth and philanthropy. First published as "Wealth," it was soon renamed "The Gospel of Wealth," and became one of the most controversial essays in American history. Following it are essays that gave his opinions on poverty, labor relations, and imperialism.

Andrew Carnegie. *Miscellaneous Writings*. Freeport, NY: Books for Libraries, 1933. Selected, organized, and edited by Carnegie scholar Burton J. Hendrick, this two-volume work includes most of the addresses and articles and "occasional" writings from Carnegie's long career. It is the most complete collection of the works that are not book-length, including both "The Gospel of Wealth" and "A Confession of Religious Faith."

Andrew Carnegie. *Triumphant Democracy.* New York: Scribner's, 1886. The first of Carnegie's books, the one whose favorable reception inspired him to continue with his writing, this began as a criticism of British monarchy but developed during its composition into a song in praise of American republicanism. Carnegie analyzed the entire American system and found it the most successful in the world and a guide to humanity's future.

Russell Conwell. *Acres of Diamonds.* Edited with a biographical sketch by Robert Shakleford. New York: Harper and Brothers, 1943. This is Pastor Conwell's famous lecture in praise of wealth, delivered thousands of times during his long and active career, first published in 1915. Shakleford's sketch details Conwell's successes as pastor of the Grace Temple Baptist Church and Temple University of Philadelphia. Further information may be found using the search term CONWELL-TEMPLE on the World Wide Web.

Eugene V. Debs. *Eugene V. Debs Speaks.* New York: Pathfinder Press, 1970. This volume contains some of Debs's greatest public addresses, among them his condemnations of Carnegie's actions at Homestead and Rockefeller's actions at Colorado.

Bill Gates. *The Road Ahead.* New York: Viking, 1995. Published at the time that Microsoft reached the heights of its power and wealth, this book is Gates's account of how he made a childhood fascination with computers into a multibillion dollar enterprise. It is obvious from reading his story that to become a wealthy entrepreneur does not require great literary or philosophical gifts.

Emma Goldman. *Living My Life,* 2 volumes. New York: Alfred A. Knopf, 1931. Goldman offered an enlightening if radical interpretation of events in the Age of Carnegie, especially Homestead. Her companion Sasha shot Henry Clay Frick.

Louis Morton Hacker. *The World of Andrew Carnegie.* Philadelphia: Lippencott, 1968. This book provides a good, factual account of Carnegie's life. His treatment of the Homestead Strike was particularly good. As the title indicates, Hacker sought to place Carnegie in his times and see nineteenth century American society through Carnegie's career.

Robert Heilbroner. "Epitaph for the Steel Master," *American Heritage,*
August 1960, pp. 4–9. Having made a study of America's industrial giants, how they accumulated their wealth and managed their
empires, Heilbroner was able in this article to capture the
essence of Carnegie's life and achievements, both positive and
negative. This is perhaps the best place to find a brief but comprehensive treatment of Carnegie the man and industrialist.

Burton Hendrick. *The Life of Andrew Carnegie,* 2 volumes. Garden
City, NJ: Doubleday, Doran, & Company, Inc., 1932. Hendrick was
one of the first Carnegie biographers. Not only did he write this
exhaustive two-volume *Life* but he also edited the two-volume
work *Miscellaneous Writings* listed previously. Hendrick omitted
nothing significant to Carnegie's life, but he interpreted events in
a manner that reflected the conservatism of the 1920s, when he
was doing his research and writing.

Warren Ilchman, Stanley Katz, and Edward Queen, editors. *Philanthropy in the World's Traditions.* Bloomington: University of
Indiana Press, 1998. As the title implies, this book covers philanthropic endeavors the world over. There is little in it about
American philanthropy; but the themes common to world philanthropy can be compared to those of the United States for a global
perspective.

Matthew Josephson. *The Robber Barons.* New York: Harcourt, Brace,
and Company, 1934. While Josephson did not invent the term
robber baron as a designation for the American industrialists of
the late nineteenth century, his book firmly inscribed it in history.
His was a wide-ranging condemnation of all the men of great
wealth whose world seemed to have collapsed in the Great
Depression of 1929. Although Carnegie was only one of the
many barons presented, his place is clarified in the context of his
era. There is plenty of information here about Carnegie and the
men who shared his place in American history.

Paul Underwood Kellogg, editor. *Wage Earning Pittsburgh,* 6 vol-
umes. This work was originally published in 1914 by the Press of
William F. Fell as a part of the series *Metropolitan America.* It
was reprinted by the Arno Press in 1974. It contains valuable
information about social, economic, and working conditions in
Carnegie's Pittsburgh. Particularly informative is the article by H.
F. J. Porter on the Carnegie mills. It also contains photographs by
Lewis Hine and drawings by Joseph Stella.

Harold Livesay. *Andrew Carnegie and the Rise of Big Business.*
Boston: Little, Brown, 1975. Reprinted by Longman, 2000.
Livesay's account of Carnegie's career is the briefest of the major
studies, yet it is comprehensive and thorough. His observations
and conclusions are among the most memorable in all of
Carnegie studies.

Walter Rauschenbusch. *Christianizing the Social Order.* New York:
Macmillan, 1912. Among the several books written by this socialist Baptist theologian, this volume best captured both Rauschenbusch's passion for reform and his social criticism. His was a rare
voice among Christian theologians, as he argued that the way to
fulfill Christ's mission in the modern world was through the col-
lectivization of wealth.

Judith Sealander. *Private Wealth and Public Life.* Baltimore: Johns
Hopkins University Press, 1997. This book deals with the foundations established for philanthropic endeavors by families of great
wealth. It places Carnegie and his enterprises in the broad context of American philanthropy, and it demonstrates the peculiari-
ties of Carnegie's philosophy and style of giving. Sealander
believes that Rockefeller's philanthropy, not Carnegie's, paved the
way toward the modern philanthropic foundation.

Donald Trump. *The Art of the Comeback.* New York: Times Books,
1997. Full of ego and self-promotion, Trump's *Art of the
Comeback* tells us more about the mentality of a contemporary
business mogul than several volumes of analysis by observers. As
does Bill Gates, Trump demonstrates that the successful entrepreneur's mind, while quick, is not deep and reflective. He and Gates
are reminders of just how unusual Carnegie, the philosophical
industrialist, actually was.

Mark Twain. "Poor Little Stephen Girard," *Carleton's Popular Readings,*
1879. The story was published in book form, illustrated for children, by Moonlight Press of London in 1980, and by Schocken of
New York in 1981. Mark Twain addressed the Horatio Alger myth
several times. In addition to this story, he wrote "The Good Little
Bad Boy" and "The Bad Little Good Boy," and his book *The Gilded
Age* dealt with the Age of Carnegie in America.

Joseph F. Wall. *Andrew Carnegie.* New York: Oxford University Press,
1970. Considered the most thorough and balanced of the
Carnegie biographies, Wall's book is still the best source for

information on Carnegie's life and work. It is factual and accurate, and in the places where Wall gives interpretation of events he is at his best. This is a long book that one wishes were even longer.

Booker T. Washington. "Atlanta Cotton and International Exposition Address," *Negro Social and Political Thought,* 1850–1920. New York: Basic Books, 1966. Washington's speech at the Atlanta Exposition was the essential message of this black educator and leader. He called on freedmen to seek economic equality before demanding social justice and on the white establishment to permit black people to work their way to this equality. This philosophy has been criticized by those who say that social and economic equality must go hand-in-hand.

CREDITS

This page constitutes an extension of the copyright page. We have made every effort to trace the ownership of all copyrighted material and to secure permission from copyright holders. In the event of any question arising as to the use of any material, we will be pleased to make the necessary corrections in future printings. Thanks are due to the following authors, publishers, and agents for permission to use the material indicated.

TEXT

p. 37, 115–116: Excerpts from p. 378–379 from *The World of Andrew Carnegie* by Louis Morton Hacker. Copyright © 1968 by Louis M. Hacker. Reprinted by permission of HarperCollins Publishers, Inc.

p. 37–38: Excerpt p. 28–31 from *Andrew Carnegie and the Rise of Big Business* by Harold C. Livesay. Copyright © 2000 by Addison-Wesley Educational Publishers, Inc. Reprinted by permission of Pearson Education.

p. 41–43: From *The Road Ahead* by Bill Gates, copyright © 1995 by William H. Gates, III. Used by permission of Viking Penguin, a division of Penguin Putnam, Inc.

p. 79–81, 152–155: From "Epitaph for a Steelmaker," *American Heritage* (August 1960), p. 4–9. Reprinted by permission of Dr. Robert Heilbroner.

p. 81–83, 116–117: From *Andrew Carnegie* by Joseph F. Wall, copyright © 1970 by Oxford University Press, Inc. Used by permission of Oxford University Press, Inc.

p. 84–86: Excerpt from *Art of Comeback* by Donald Trump. New York: Times Books, 1997.

p. 119: Copyright 1981 U. S. News & World Report, L. P. Reprinted with permission.

PHOTO

xvii   © CORBIS
p. 9   Brown Brothers, Sterling, PA.
p. 11   Brown Brothers, Sterling, PA.
p. 48   Brown Brothers, Sterling, PA.